The Institute of Certified Bookk

Level I

CERTIFICATE IN BASIC BOOKKEEPING

REVISION KIT

British Library Cataloguing-in-Publication Data

A catalogue record for this book is available from the British Library.

Published by:
Kaplan Publishing UK
Unit 2 The Business Centre
Molly Millars Lane
Wokingham
RG41 2QZ
ISBN 978-0-85732-779-6

© Kaplan Financial Limited, 2012

Printed and bound in Great Britain

All rights reserved. No part of this publication may be reproduced, stored in a retrieval system, or transmitted, in any form or by any means, electronic, mechanical, photocopying, recording or otherwise, without the prior written permission of Kaplan Publishing.

The text in this material and any others made available by any Kaplan Group company does not amount to advice on a particular matter and should not be taken as such. No reliance should be placed on the content as the basis for any investment or other decision or in connection with any advice given to third parties. Please consult your appropriate professional adviser as necessary. Kaplan Publishing Limited and all other Kaplan group companies expressly disclaim all liability to any person in respect of any losses or other claims, whether direct, indirect, incidental, consequential or otherwise arising in relation to the use of such materials.

INDEX TO QUESTIONS AND ANSWERS

Page number

	Question	Answers
BUSINESS DOCUMENTS	1	71
BOOKS OF ORIGINAL ENTRY	12	75
LEDGER ACCOUNTS AND THE DIVISION OF THE LEDGER	28	81
MAKING AND RECEIVING PAYMENTS	40	90
THE TRIAL BALANCE	55	100
UNDERPINNING KNOWLEDGE	63	107

Workbook Preface

This workbook has been written for level I of the Institute of Certified Bookkeepers (ICB) examination structure.

It is designed to complement the corresponding ICB study text which contains the detailed syllabus coverage. The chapters in this workbook relate exactly to the level I syllabus and are designed to consolidate knowledge in each of these areas.

Section 1

PRACTICE QUESTIONS

BUSINESS DOCUMENTS

1 NAN NURSING

A supply of chocolate puddings has been delivered to Nan Nursing by Pudding and Co. The purchase order sent from Nan Nursing, and the invoice from Pudding and Co, are shown below.

Nan Nursing
22 Nursery Road
Keighley, BD22 7BD
Purchase Order No. HH72

To: Pudding and Co

Date: 15 August 20XX

Please supply 50 chocolate puddings product code 742087

Purchase price: £20 per 10, plus VAT

Discount: less 10% trade discount, as agreed.

Pudding and Co
17 Pudding Lane, Bradford, BD19 7HX
VAT Registration No. 234 7654 00
Invoice No. 428

Nan Nursing
22 Nursery Road
Keighley, BD22 7BD

20 August 20XX

50 .... chocolate puddings product code 742087 @ £2 each	£50
Less Trade Discount	£10
Net	£40
VAT	£ 8
Total	£48

Terms: 30 days net

LEVEL I: CERTIFICATE IN BASIC BOOKKEEPING

Check the invoice against the purchase order and answer the following questions.

Has the correct purchase price of the chocolate puddings been charged?   Y / N

Has the correct total discount, as agreed with the client, been calculated?   Y / N

What would be the VAT amount charged if the invoice was correct?   £_____

What would be the total amount charged if the invoice was correct?   £_____

2 ALESSANDRO LTD

On 1 Aug Alessandro Ltd delivered the following goods to a credit customer, Palermo Wholesale

---

Alessandro Ltd
8 Alan Street
Glasgow, G1 7DJ

Delivery note No. 24369

01 Aug 20XX

Palermo Wholesale   Customer account code: AGG42
17 Zoo Lane
Dartford
DH8 4TJ

40 standard baths, product code SB05

The list price of the goods was £62.50 each plus VAT. Palermo Wholesale is to be given a 12% trade discount and a 5% discount if they pay within 30 days.

(a) **Complete the invoice below.**

Alessandro Ltd
8 Alan Street
Glasgow, G1 7DJ
VAT Registration No. 398 2774 01

Palermo Wholesale   Customer account code:
17 Zoo Lane
Dartford
DH8 4TJ   Delivery note number:
                                               Date: 1 Aug 20XX
Invoice No: 327

Quantity	Product code	Total list price £	Net amount after discount £	VAT £	Gross £

(b) Alessandro Ltd offers each customer a discount of 5% if they pay within 30 days. What is the name of this type of discount?

3 ALPHA LTD

A supply of paper has been delivered to Alpha Ltd by Pixie Paper. The purchase order sent from Alpha Ltd, and the invoice from Pixie Paper, are shown below.

Alpha Ltd
121 Baker St
Newcastle, NE1 7DJ

Purchase Order No. PO1792

To: Pixie Paper

Date: 5 Aug 20XX

Please supply 50 boxes of A4 paper product code 16257

Purchase price: £10 per box, plus VAT

Discount: less 10% trade discount, as agreed.

Pixie Paper
24 Eden Terrace, Durham, DH9 7TE
VAT Registration No. 464 392 401

Invoice No. 1679

Alpha Ltd
121 Baker St
Newcastle, NE1 7DJ
9 Aug 20XX

50 boxes of A4 paper, product code 16257 @ £10 each	£500
VAT	£100
Total	£600

Terms: 30 days net

Check the invoice against the purchase order and answer the following questions.

Has the correct product been supplied by Pixie Paper?	Y / N
Has the correct net price been calculated?	Y / N
Is the total invoice price correct?	Y / N
What would be the VAT amount charged if the invoice was correct?	£_____
What would be the total amount charged if the invoice was correct?	£_____

4 ABG LTD

Shown below is a statement of account received from a credit supplier, and the supplier's account as shown in the purchases ledger of Alpha Ltd.

ABG Ltd

14 Hassle Street, Durham, DH9 7RQ

To: Alpha Ltd

121 Baker St

Newcastle, NE1 7DJ

STATEMENT OF ACCOUNT

Date 20XX	Invoice Number	Details	Invoice Amount £	Cheque Amount £	Balance £
1 May	468	Goods	7,600		7,600
1 June		Cheque		2,500	5,100
5 June	472	Goods	4,200		9,300
12 June	478	Goods	500		9,800
22 June	486	Goods	1,680		11,480
30 June		Cheque		2,000	9,480

ABG Ltd

Date 20XX	Details	Amount £	Date 20XX	Details	Amount £
4 June	Bank	2,500	3 May	Purchases	7,600
28 June	Bank	2,000	8 June	Purchases	4,200
28 July	Purchase return	900	15 June	Purchases	500

(a) Which item is missing from the statement of account from ABG Ltd?

[ ]

(b) Which item is missing from the supplier's account in Alpha Ltd's purchases ledger?

[ ]

(c) Once the omitted items have been recorded, what is the agreed balance outstanding between Alpha Ltd and ABG Ltd?

£ [ ]

PRACTICE QUESTIONS: SECTION 1

5 KEYBOARD SUPPLIES

You have been given details of goods that have been returned to Keyboard Supplies. The return has been checked and authorised and you are now to prepare the credit note.

Return from: H H Music   SL 09
              Tenant House   Trade discount 15%
              Perley
              TN7 8ER

Goods returned: 1 Bento keyboard   Code B3060   Unit price (before VAT and discount) £126.00

Reason for return: Goods not ordered

Today's date is 17 April 20X1 and the last credit note to have been issued was CN 0336.

Required:

Prepare the credit note on the blank credit note given below.

CREDIT NOTE

Credit Note to:

Keyboard Supplies
Trench Park Estate
Fieldham
Sussex TN21 4AF
Tel: 01829 654545
Fax: 01829 654646

Credit Note no:
Tax point:
VAT reg no: 466 1128 30
Your reference:
Purchase order no:

Code	Description	Quantity	VAT rate %	Unit price £	Amount exclusive of VAT £

Trade discount   %

VAT at 20%
Total amount

6   ELECTRONIC KEYBOARDS

You work in the accounts department of Keyboard Supplies, a supplier of a wide range of electronic keyboards to a variety of music shops on credit. Given below is a purchase order which is due to be despatched today.

You also have the following extract from the customer master file:

Customer	Sales ledger code	Trade discount	Settlement discount
Musicolor Ltd	SL06	10%	3% – 10 days

Today's date is 17 April 20X1 and the last sales invoice to be sent out was invoice number 06112. Normal credit terms are 30 days although some customers are offered a settlement discount. The business is registered for VAT and all of the goods are standard rated.

Required:

Complete the sales invoices for this sale on the blank invoice supplied.

PURCHASE ORDER

Musicolor Ltd
23 High Street
Nutford
Sussex TN11 4TZ
Tel: 01826 434111
Fax: 01826 434112
Date: 12 April 20X1
Purchase order no: 04318

To: Keyboard Supplies
Trench Park Estate
Fieldham
Sussex TN21 4AF

Delivery address
(If different from above)

Invoice address
(If different from above)

Code	Quantity	Description	Unit price (exclusive of VAT and discounts) £
Z4600	2	Zanni Keyboard	185.00
A4802	3	Atol Keyboard	130.00

INVOICE

Invoice to:

Keyboard Supplies
Trench Park Estate
Fieldham
Sussex TN21 4AF
Tel: 01829 654545
Fax: 01829 654646

Deliver to:

Invoice no:
Tax point:
VAT reg no: 466 1128 30
Your reference:
Purchase order no:

Code	Description	Quantity	VAT rate %	Unit price £	Amount exclusive of VAT £

Trade discount   %
VAT at 20%
Total amount payable

7 FARMHOUSE PICKLES LTD

You work in the accounts department of Farmhouse Pickles Ltd and given below are two debtors' accounts from the subsidiary sales ledger.

Grant & Co   **SL07**

		£			£
1 April	Balance b/d	337.69	12 April	SRDB – 0335	38.70
4 April	SDB 32656	150.58	20 April	CRB	330.94
18 April	SDB 32671	179.52	20 April	CRB – discount	6.75
25 April	SDB 32689	94.36	24 April	SRDB – 0346	17.65

Mitchell Partners   **SL10**

		£			£
1 April	Balance b/d	180.46	12 April	SRDB – 0344	66.89
7 April	SDB 32662	441.57	21 April	CRB	613.58
20 April	SDB 32669	274.57	21 April	CRB – discount	8.45

Required:

Prepare statements to be sent to each of these customers at the end of April 20X1 on the blank statements provided.

	Farmhouse Pickles Ltd
	225 School Lane
	Weymouth
	Dorset
	WE36 5NR
Tel:	0261 480444
Fax:	0261 480555
Date:	

To:

STATEMENT

Date	Transaction	Debit £	Credit £	Balance £

May we remind you that our credit terms are 30 days

	Farmhouse Pickles Ltd
	225 School Lane
	Weymouth
	Dorset
	WE36 5NR
Tel:	0261 480444
Fax:	0261 480555
Date:	

To:

STATEMENT

Date	Transaction	Debit £	Credit £	Balance £

May we remind you that our credit terms are 30 days

PRACTICE QUESTIONS: SECTION 1

8 NETHAN BUILDERS

You work in the accounts department of Nethan Builders. The invoice, purchase order and delivery note related to a specific purchase are presented below.

Required:

Check the paperwork carefully and note any errors or discrepancies that you find.

INVOICE

Invoice to:
Nethan Builders
Brecon House
Stamford Road
Manchester
M16 4PL

Deliver to:
As above

Jenson Ltd
30 Longfield Park
Kingsway
M45 2TP
Tel: 0161 511 4666
Fax: 0161 511 4777

Invoice no: 47792
Tax point: 22 April 20X1
VAT reg no: 641 3229 45
Purchase order no: 7162

Code	Description	Quantity	VAT rate %	Unit price £	Amount exclusive of VAT £
PL432115	Door lining set 32 × 115 mm	14	20%	33.15	464.10
PL432140	Door lining set 32 × 138 mm	8	20%	30.25	242.00

	706.10
Trade discount 15%	105.92
	600.18
VAT at 20%	120.03
Total amount payable	720.21

Deduct discount of 3% if paid within 14 days.

	PURCHASE ORDER		

Nethan Builders

Brecon House
Stamford Road
Manchester
M16 4PL
Tel: 0161 521 6411
Fax: 0161 521 6412
Date: 14 April 20X1
Purchase order no: 7162

To: Jenson Ltd
30 Longfield Park
Kingsway
M45 2TP

Delivery address
(If different from above)
—

Invoice address
(If different from above)
—

Code	Quantity	Description	Unit price (exclusive of VAT) £
PL432140	8	Door lining set 32 × 138 mm	33.15
PL432115	15	Door lining set 32 × 115 mm	30.25

DELIVERY NOTE

Deliver to:
Nethan Builders
Brecon House
Stamford Road
Manchester
M16 4PL

Jenson Ltd
30 Longfield Park
Kingsway
M45 2TP
Tel: 0161 511 4666
Fax: 0161 511 4777
Delivery note no: 771460
Date: 19 April 20X1
VAT reg no: 641 3229 45

Code	Description	Quantity	VAT rate %	Unit price £	Amount exclusive of VAT £
PL432115	Door lining set 32 × 115 mm	14			
PL432140	Door lining set 32 × 138 mm	8			

Goods received in good condition.

Print name C JULIAN
Signature   C Julian
Date   19/4/X1

Discrepancies:

1
2
3

BOOKS OF ORIGINAL ENTRY

9 Calculate the VAT on the following sales:

(a) A sale for £140.00 excluding VAT.

(b) A sale for £560.00 net of VAT.

(c) A sale for £780.00 including VAT.

(d) A sale for £970.00 including VAT.

10 Calculate the VAT on the following sales:

(a) A sale for £280.00 excluding VAT where a settlement discount of 2% is offered.

(b) A sale for £480.00 excluding VAT where a trade discount of 3% is offered.

(c) A sale for £800.00 net of VAT where an early payment discount of 5% is offered but not taken.

(d) A sale of £650.00 excluding VAT where a settlement discount of 4% is offered but not taken.

11 ARISTOTLE

Aristotle sells £600 of goods, exclusive of VAT, to Bairstow. Aristotle offers Bairstow a settlement discount of 3%. Calculate the amount that Bairstow will pay Aristotle if:

(a) Bairstow takes the settlement discount; and

(b) Bairstow does not take the settlement discount.

12 AARDVARK

Aardvark sells £700 of goods to Christie net of VAT. Aardvark offers Christie a settlement discount of 5%. Calculate the total of the sale to be entered into the main/general ledger and the total payment due from Christie, assuming:

(a) Christie takes the settlement discount; and

(b) Christie does not take the settlement discount.

13 SALES DAY BOOK

Sales invoices have been prepared and partially entered in the sales day-book, as shown below.

(a) Complete the entries in the sales day-book by inserting the appropriate figures for each invoice.

(b) Total the last five columns of the sales day-book.

Sales day-book

Date 20XX	Details	Invoice number	Total £	VAT £	Net £	Sales type 1 £	Sales type 2 £
31 Dec	Poonams	105	3,600	600	3000		3,000
31 Dec	D Taylor	106	7680	1,280	6400	6,400	
31 Dec	Smiths	107	3,840	640	3,200		3,200
	Totals		15120	2,520	12,600	6400	6200

14 LADY LTD

Given below is the purchases day book for Lady Ltd

Date	Invoice No.	Code	Supplier	Total	VAT	Net
1 Dec	03582	PL210	M Brown	300.00	50.00	250.00
5 Dec	03617	PL219	H Madden	183.55	30.59	152.96
7 Dec	03622	PL227	L Singh	132.60	22.10	110.50
10 Dec	03623	PL228	A Stevens	90.00	15.00	75.00
18 Dec	03712	PL301	N Shema	197.08	32.84	164.24
			TOTALS	**903.23**	**150.53**	**752.70**

Required:

(a) Post the totals of the purchases day book to the main/general ledger accounts given;

(b) Post the invoices to the creditors' accounts in the subsidiary ledger given.

General ledger

Purchases ledger control account

	£		£
		1 Dec Balance b/d	5,103.90
		18 Dec PDB	903-23

VAT account

	£		£
18 DEC PDB	150-53	1 Dec Balance b/d	526.90

Purchases account

	£		£
1 Dec balance b/d	22,379.52		
18 DEC PDB	752-70		

Subsidiary Ledger

M Brown

	£		£
		1 Dec Balance b/d	68.50
		1 Dec PDB 03582	300-00

H Madden

	£		£
		1 Dec Balance b/d	286.97
		5 DEC PDB 03617	183-55

L Singh

	£		£
		1 Dec Balance b/d	125.89
		7 DEC 03622	132-60

A Stevens

	£		£
		1 Dec Balance b/d	12.36
		10 DEC PDB 03623	90

N Shema

	£		£
		1 Dec Balance b/d	168.70
		18 DEC PDB 03712	197-08

15 BUTTONS LTD

The following transactions all took place on 31 July and have been entered into the purchases day book of Buttons Ltd as shown below. No entries have yet been made into the ledger system.

Date 20XX	Details	Invoice number	Total £	VAT £	Net £
31 July	Peak & Co	1720	6,240	1,040	5,200
31 July	Max Ltd	1721	12,720	2,120	10,600
31 July	McIntyre Wholesale	1722	5,760	960	4,800
31 July	Pigmy Ltd	1723	3,744	624	3,120
	Totals		28,464	4,744	23,720

(a) What will be the entries in the purchases ledger?

Account name	Amount £	Debit ✓	Credit ✓
Peak & Co	6240		✓
Max Ltd	12720		✓
McIntyre Wholesale	5,760		✓
Pigmy Ltd	3744		✓

(b) What will be the entries in the general ledger?

Account name	Amount £	Debit ✓	Credit ✓
PLCA	28464		✓
VAT	4744	✓	
Purchases	23720	✓	

PRACTICE QUESTIONS: SECTION 1

16 FREDDIE LTD

Purchase invoices have been received and partially entered in the purchases day-book of Freddie Ltd, as shown below.

(a) Complete the first two entries in the purchases day-book by inserting the appropriate figures for each invoice.

(b) Complete the final entry in the purchases day book by inserting the appropriate figures from the following invoice.

Novot & Co
5 Pheasant Way, Essex, ES9 8BN
VAT Registration No. 453 098 541

Invoice No. 2176

Freddie Ltd
9 Banbury Street
Sheffield
31 July 20XX

10 boxes of product code 14212 @ £400 each	£4,000
VAT	£800
Total	£4,800
Payment terms 30 days	

Purchases day-book

Date 20XX	Details	Invoice number	Total £	VAT £	Net £	Product 14211 £	Product 14212 £
31 July	Box Ltd	SI063	960	160	800	800	
31 July	Shrew Ltd	367FL	14,400	2,400	12,000	12,000	
31 July	Novot & Co	2176	4,800	800	4,000		4,000
	Totals		20,160	3,360	16,800	12,800	4,000

LEVEL I: CERTIFICATE IN BASIC BOOKKEEPING

17   LOUIS LTD

The following transactions all took place on 31 Jan and have been entered into the sales day book of Louis Ltd as shown below. No entries have yet been made into the ledger system.

Date 20XX	Details	Invoice number	Total £	VAT £	Net £
31 Jan	Sheep & Co	1400	3,840	640	3,200
31 Jan	Cow Ltd	1401	11,760	1,960	9,800
31 Jan	Chicken & Partners	1402	6,720	1,120	5,600
31 Jan	Pig Ltd	1403	14,496	2,416	12,080
	Totals		36,816	6,136	30,680

(a)   What will be the entries in the sales ledger?

Account name	Amount £	Debit ✓	Credit ✓
Sheep & Co	3840	✓	
Cow Ltd	11,760	✓	
Chicken & Partners	6,720	✓	
Pig Ltd	14,496	✓	

(b)   What will be the entries in the general ledger?

Account name	Amount £	Debit ✓	Credit ✓
SLCA	38,816	✓	
VAT	6136		✓
Sales	30,680		✓

18   RING RING TELEPHONE'S

The following is an extract from Ring Ring Telephone's books of prime entry.

	Totals for quarter		
Sales day-book		**Purchases day-book**	
Net	£153,000	Net:	£81,000
VAT:	£30,600	VAT:	£16,200
Gross:	£183,600	Gross:	£97,200
Sales returns day-book		**Purchases returns day-book**	
Net:	£1,800	Net:	£5,800
VAT:	£360	VAT:	£1,160
Gross:	£2,160	Gross:	£6,960
Cash book			
Net cash sales:	£240		
VAT:	£48		
Gross cash sales:	£288		

PRACTICE QUESTIONS: SECTION 1

(a) Complete the VAT control account to reflect the transactions in the quarter?

DR   VAT control   CR

Details	Amount £	Details	Amount £
SRDB	360	SDB	30,600
PDB	16,200	CRB	48
		PRDB	1,160
bal c/d	15,248		
	31,808		31,808
		bal b/d	15,248

(b) The VAT return has been completed and shows an amount owing from the tax authorities of £15,248.

Is the VAT return correct?   Yes / **No**

19   D F ENGINEERING

You work in the accounts department of D F Engineering and one of your tasks is to write up the day books.

Given below are the details of the sales invoices that have been issued this week. D F Engineering does not offer trade or settlement discounts but is registered for VAT and all sales are of standard rated goods.

Invoices sent out:

20X1		Code	£		Invoice number
1 May	Fraser & Co	SL14	128.68	plus VAT	03466
	Letterhead Ltd	SL03	257.90	plus VAT	03467
2 May	Jeliteen Traders	SL15	96.58	plus VAT	03468
3 May	Harper Bros	SL22	268.15	plus VAT	03469
	Juniper Ltd	SL17	105.38	plus VAT	03470
4 May	H G Frank	SL30	294.67	plus VAT	03471
5 May	Keller Assocs	SL07	110.58	plus VAT	03472

KAPLAN PUBLISHING

LEVEL I: CERTIFICATE IN BASIC BOOKKEEPING

Required:

Write up the sales day book given for the week ending 5 May 20X1 and total all of the columns.

Sales day book						
Date	Invoice No	Customer name	Code	Total	VAT	Net
				£	£	£

20 KEYBOARD SUPPLIES

You work in the accounts department of Keyboard Supplies, a supplier of a wide range of electronic keyboards to a variety of music shops on credit. Given below are three sales invoices that you have just sent out to customers and these are to be written up into the sales day book given below.

Sales of four different types of keyboard are made and the sales are analysed into each of these four types and coded as follows:

Atol keyboards   01

Bento keyboards   02

Garland keyboards   03

Zanni keyboards   04

PRACTICE QUESTIONS: SECTION 1

Required:

Write up the analysed sales day book and total each of the columns.

INVOICE

Invoice to:	Keyboard Supplies
B Z S Music	Trench Park Estate
42 Westhill	Fieldham
Nutford TN11 3PQ	Sussex TN21 4AF
	Tel: 01829 654545
	Fax: 01829 654646

Deliver to:	Invoice no:	06116
As above	Tax point:	18 April 20X1
	VAT reg no:	466 1128 30
	Your reference:	SL01
	Purchase order no:	77121

Code	Description	Quantity	VAT rate %	Unit price £	Amount exclusive of VAT £
B4012	Bento Keyboard	3	20	180.00	540.00
Z2060	Zanni Keyboard	6	20	164.00	984.00
					1,524.00
Trade discount 20%					304.80
					1,219.20
VAT at 20%					236.52
Total amount payable					1,455.72

Deduct discount of 3% if paid within 10 days, net 30 days

INVOICE

Invoice to:
M T Retail
Fraser House
Perley TN7 8QT

Keyboard Supplies
Trench Park Estate
Fieldham
Sussex TN21 4AF
Tel: 01829 654545
Fax: 01829 654646

Deliver to:
As above

Invoice no:	06117
Tax point:	18 April 20X1
VAT reg no:	466 1128 30
Your reference:	SL29
Purchase order no:	P04648

Code	Description	Quantity	VAT rate %	Unit price £	Amount exclusive of VAT £
A6060	Atol Keyboard	1	20	210.00	210.00
Z4080	Zanni Keyboard	1	20	325.00	325.00
					535.00
VAT at 20%					107.00
Total amount payable					642.00

Net 30 days

INVOICE

Invoice to:
Harmer & Co
1 Acre Street
Nutford TN11 6HA

Deliver to:
As above

Keyboard Supplies
Trench Park Estate
Fieldham
Sussex TN21 4AF
Tel: 01829 654545
Fax: 01829 654646

Invoice no:	06118
Tax point:	18 April 20X1
VAT reg no:	466 1128 30
Your reference:	SL17
Purchase order no:	047721

Code	Description	Quantity	VAT rate %	Unit price £	Amount exclusive of VAT £
G4326	Garland Keyboard	3	20	98.00	294.00
B2040	Bento Keyboard	5	20	115.00	575.00
					869.00
VAT at 20%					168.59
Total amount payable					1,037.59

Deduct discount of 3% if paid within 10 days, net 30 days

Sales day book

Date	Invoice No	Customer name	Code	Total £	VAT £	01 £	02 £	03 £	04 £
18/4/20XX	06117	MT RETAIL	SL29	642	107	210			325
18/4/20XX	06118	HARMER+CO	SL17	1037.59	168.59		575	294	
18/4/20XX	06116	BZS Music	SL01	1455.72	236.52		432		787.2
				3135.31	512.11	210	1007	294	1112.20

21   NETHAN BUILDERS PURCHASE INVOICES

Nethan Builders analyse their purchases into wood, bricks and cement, and small consumables such as nails and screws. You are given three purchase invoices, recently received, to enter into the purchases day book given.

An extract from the purchase ledger coding manual is given:

Supplier	Purchase ledger code
A J Broom & Co Ltd	PL08
Jenson Ltd	PL13
Magnum Supplies	PL16

Today's date is 3 May 20X1.

Enter the invoices into the analysed purchases day book and total each of the columns.

INVOICE

Magnum Supplies

140/150 Park Estate
Manchester
M20 6EG
Tel: 0161 561 3202
Fax: 0161 561 3200

Invoice to:
Nethan Builders
Brecon House
Stamford Road
Manchester
M16 4PL

Deliver to:
As above

Invoice no:	077401
Tax point:	1 May 20X1
VAT reg no:	611 4337 90

Code	Description	Quantity	VAT rate %	Unit price £	Amount exclusive of VAT £
BH47732	House Bricks – Red	400	20%	1.24	496.00
					496.00
					74.40
					421.60
					82.63
					504.23

Trade discount 15%

VAT at 20%

Total amount payable

Deduct discount of 2% if paid within 10 days

INVOICE

AJ Broom & Company Limited

Invoice to:
Nethan Builders
Brecon House
Stamford Road
Manchester
M16 4PL

59 Parkway
Manchester
M2 6EG
Tel: 0161 560 3392
Fax: 0161 560 5322

Deliver to:
As above

Invoice no: 046193
Tax point: 1 May 20X1
VAT reg no: 661 2359 07

Code	Description	Quantity	VAT rate %	Unit price £	Amount exclusive of VAT £
DGT472	SDGS Softwood 47 × 225 mm	11.2 m	20%	8.44	94.53
NBD021	Oval Wire Nails 100 mm	7 boxes	20%	2.50	17.50

	112.03
Trade discount 10%	11.20
	100.83
VAT at 20%	20.17
Total amount payable	121.00

INVOICE

Jenson Ltd

Invoice to:
Nethan Builders
Brecon House
Stamford Road
Manchester
M16 4PL

30 Longfield Park
Kingsway
M45 2TP
Tel: 0161 511 4666
Fax: 0161 511 4777

Deliver to:
As above

Invoice no:	47823
Tax point:	1 May 20X1
VAT reg no:	641 3229 45
Purchase order no:	7211

Code	Description	Quantity	VAT rate %	Unit price £	Amount exclusive of VAT £
PLY8FU	Plywood Hardboard	16 sheets	20%	17.80	284.80
BU611	Ventilator Brick	10	20%	8.60	86.00
					370.80

VAT at 20% — 71.94
Total amount payable — 442.74
Deduct discount of 3% if paid within 14 days

Purchases day book								
Date	Inv. no	Code	Supplier	Total	VAT	Wood	Bricks/Cement	Consumables

PRACTICE QUESTIONS: SECTION 1

22 NETHAN BUILDERS CREDIT NOTES

Nethan Builders have recently received the three credit notes given. They are to be recorded in the analysed purchases returns day book given.

An extract from the purchase ledger coding manual shows:

Supplier	Purchase ledger code
Jenson Ltd	PL13
Haddow Bros	PL03
Magnum Supplies	PL16

Today's date is 3 May 20X1.

You are required to enter the credit notes into the analysed purchases returns day book and to total each of the columns.

CREDIT NOTE

Credit note to:
Nethan Builders
Brecon House
Stamford Road
Manchester
M16 4PL

Jenson Ltd
30 Longfield Park
Kingsway
M45 2TP
Tel: 0161 511 4666
Fax: 0161 511 4777

Credit note no: CN06113
Tax point: 28 April 20X1
VAT reg no: 641 3229 45
Sales invoice no: 47792

Code	Description	Quantity	VAT rate %	Unit price £	Amount exclusive of VAT £
PL432115	Door Lining Set – Wood 32 × 115 mm	1	20%	30.25	30.25

	30.25
Trade discount 15%	4.54
	25.71
VAT at 20%	5.14
Total amount of credit	30.85

CREDIT NOTE

Credit note to:
Nethan Builders
Brecon House
Stamford Road
Manchester
M16 4PL

Haddow Bros
The White House
Standing Way
Manchester
M13 6FH
Tel: 0161 560 3140
Fax: 0161 560 6140

Credit note no: 06132
Tax point: 27 April 20X1
VAT reg no: 460 3559 71

Code	Description	Quantity	VAT rate %	Unit price £	Amount exclusive of VAT £
PLY8FE1	Plywood Hardwood 2440 × 1220 mm	2	20%	17.80	35.60
					35.60
VAT at 20%					7.12
Total amount of credit					42.72

CREDIT NOTE

Credit note to:
Nethan Builders
Brecon House
Stamford Road
Manchester
M16 4PL

Magnum Supplies
140/150 Park Estate
Manchester
M20 6EG
Tel: 0161 561 3202
Fax: 0161 561 3200

Credit note no: C4163
Tax point: 30 April 20X1
VAT reg no: 611 4337 90

Code	Description	Quantity	VAT rate %	Unit price £	Amount exclusive of VAT £
BU1628	Ventilator Brick	5	20%	9.20	46.00

	46.00
Trade discount 15%	6.90
	39.10
VAT at 20%	7.82
Total amount of credit	46.92

Purchases returns day book

Date	Credit note no	Code	Supplier	Total	VAT	Wood	Bricks/ Cement	Consumables

LEVEL I: CERTIFICATE IN BASIC BOOKKEEPING

LEDGER ACCOUNTS AND THE DIVISION OF THE LEDGER

23 ANNAND

Annand makes the following cash transactions:

(a) Pays £5,000 into the bank as capital.

(b) Buys goods for £800.

(c) Pays rent of £500.

(d) Buys a van for £2,000.

(e) Sells some of the goods for £600.

(f) Sells some more of the goods for £700.

(g) Buys goods for £1,000.

(h) Buys stationery for £200.

(i) Takes £500 out of the bank as drawings.

Prepare the main/general ledger accounts for Annand, reflecting the transactions disclosed above.

24 BERYL

Beryl makes the following cash transactions:

(a) Pays £4,000 into the bank as capital.

(b) Buys goods for £700.

(c) Buys champagne to entertain the staff for £300.

(d) Purchases three computers for £3,000.

(e) Sells goods for £1,500.

(f) Draws £500 cash.

(g) Purchases goods for £1,200.

(h) Pays telephone bill of £600.

(i) Receives telephone bill rebate of £200.

(j) Buys stationery for £157.

Prepare the main/general ledger accounts for Beryl, reflecting the transactions disclosed above.

25 WIGGLE POGGLE LTD

The following two accounts are in the main/general ledger of Wiggle Poggle Ltd at the close of day on 31 July.

(a) Insert the balance carried down together with date and details.

(b) Insert the totals.

(c) Insert the balance brought down together with date and details.

Discount Allowed

Date 20XX	Details	Amount £	Date 20XX	Details	Amount £
01 July	Balance b/d	1,560			
14 July	Sales ledger control account (SLCA)	480			
16 July	Sales ledger control account (SLCA)	120			
	Total			Total	

Interest Income

Date 20XX	Details	Amount £	Date 20XX	Details	Amount £
			01 July	Balance b/d	320
			28 July	Bank	80
	Total			Total	

26 INTREPID INTERIORS

Intrepid Interiors has started a new business, Intrepid Exteriors, and a new set of accounts are to be opened. A partially completed journal to record the opening entries is shown below.

Record the journal entries needed in the accounts in the general ledger of Intrepid Exteriors to deal with the opening entries.

Account name	Amount £	Debit ✓	Credit ✓
Cash at bank	7,250		
Bank Loan	5,000		
Capital	10,625		
Motor Vehicles	4,750		
Insurances	575		
Stationery	300		
Sundry expenses	225		
Motor expenses	135		
Advertising	990		
Rent and rates	1,400		

27 MONSTER MUNCHIES

This is a summary of transactions with customers of Monster Munchies during the month of June.

(a) Show whether each entry will be a debit or credit in the sales ledger control account in the main/general ledger.

Details	Amount £	Debit ✓	Credit ✓
Balance of debtors at 1 June	48,000		
Goods sold on credit	12,415		
Receipts from credit customers	22,513		
Discounts allowed	465		
Sales returns from credit customers	320		

(b) What will be the balance brought down on 1 July on the above account?

Dr £37,117	
Cr £37,117	
Dr £83,713	
Cr £83,713	
Dr £58,883	
Cr £58,883	

The following debit balances were in the sales ledger on 1 July.

	£
XXX Ltd	21,300
Brittle Homes Ltd	5,376
Colin and Campbell	333
Bashford Incorporated	1,733
Mainstreet Homes	3,426
Shamrock Interiors	4,629

(c) Reconcile the balances shown above with the sales ledger control account balance you have calculated in part (a).

	£
Sales ledger control account balance as at 30 June	
Total of sales ledger accounts as at 30 June	
Difference	

(d) What may have caused the difference you calculated in part (b)?

Sales returns may have been omitted from the subsidiary ledger	
Discounts allowed may have been omitted from the subsidiary ledger	
Sales returns may have been entered in the subsidiary ledger x 2	
Discounts allowed may have been entered in the subsidiary ledger x 2	

28 CILLA'S SINKS

This is a summary of transactions with suppliers of Cilla's Sinks during the month of June.

(a) Show whether each entry will be a debit or credit in the purchases ledger control account (PLCA) in the main/general ledger.

Details	Amount £	Debit ✓	Credit ✓
Balance of creditors at 1 June	52,150		
Goods bought on credit	19,215		
Payments made to credit suppliers	19,073		
Discounts received	284		
Goods returned to credit suppliers	1,023		

(b) What will be the balance brought down on 1 July on the above account?

	✓
Dr £51,553	
Cr £51,553	
Dr £50,985	
Cr £50,985	
Dr £50,701	
Cr £50,701	

The following credit balances were in the purchases ledger on 1 July.

	£
BWF Ltd	19,563
All Parts Ltd	10,207
Hove Albion	4,501
Barton Groves	6,713
Cambridge Irons	5,913
Outside Arenas	5,111

(c) Reconcile the balances shown above with the purchases ledger control account balance you have calculated in part (a).

	£
Purchases ledger control account balance as at 30 June	
Total of purchases ledger accounts as at 30 June	
Difference	

(d) What may have caused the difference you calculated in part (b)?

	✓
Goods returned may have been omitted from the subsidiary ledger	
Discounts received may have been omitted from the subsidiary ledger	
Goods returned may have been entered in the subsidiary ledger x 2	
Discounts received may have been entered in the subsidiary ledger x 2	

29 BANK LEDGER

The following bank ledger has been written up for the month of May 20X4. There was no opening balance.

Bank

	£		£
Capital	10,000	Computer	1,000
Sales	2,000	Telephone	567
Sales	3,000	Rent	1,500
Sales	2,000	Rates	125
		Stationery	247
		Petrol	49
		Purchases	2,500
		Drawings	500
		Petrol	42

(a) Close the bank ledger for the year, showing the debit and credit totals and show the balance carried down at the end of the year.

(b) Does the closing balance represent a positive bank balance or an overdrawn balance?

Positive / Overdrawn

LEVEL I: CERTIFICATE IN BASIC BOOKKEEPING

30 SALES DAY BOOK

Given below is a completed sales day book for the week ending 26 April 20X1.

Required:

Post the totals of the sales day book to the main/general ledger accounts and post each individual invoice to the subsidiary ledger (sales ledger) accounts.

Sales day book

Date	Invoice No	Customer name	Code	Total £	VAT £	Net £
20X1						
22 April	4671	J T Howard	SL15	141.89	23.65	118.24
22 April	4672	F Parker	SL07	101.18	16.86	84.32
23 April	4673	Harlow Ltd	SL02	127.76	21.29	106.47
24 April	4674	Edmunds & Co	SL13	171.32	28.55	142.77
26 April	4675	Peters & Co	SL09	115.45	19.24	96.21
				657.60	109.59	548.01

Main ledger accounts

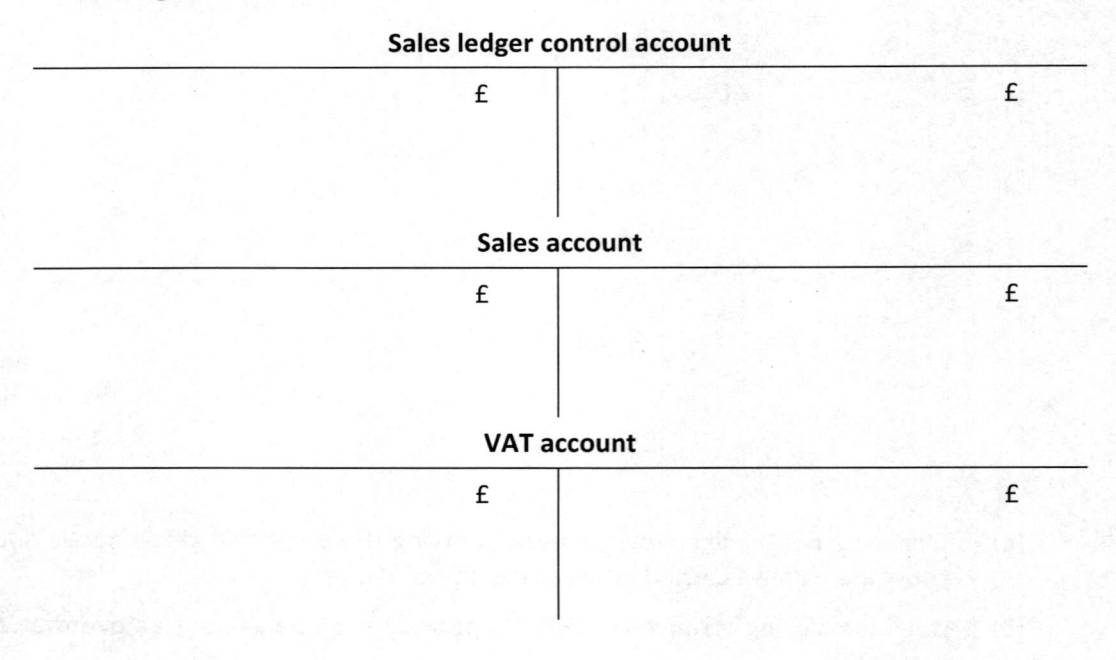

Sales ledger control account

£	£

Sales account

£	£

VAT account

£	£

Subsidiary ledger accounts

J T Howard			SL15
£			£

F Parker			SL07
£			£

Harlow Ltd			SL02
£			£

Edmunds & Co			SL13
£			£

Peters & Co			SL09
£			£

31 SALES DAY BOOK (2)

Given below is a sales returns day book for the month of April.

Required:

Post the totals to the main/general ledger accounts and post the individual entries to the subsidiary ledger accounts.

Sales returns day book						
Date	Credit note No	Customer name	Code	Total	VAT	Sales Returns
				£	£	£
20X1						
7/4	2114	Gerard & Co	G01	35.10	5.85	29.25
15/4	2115	Filmer Ltd	F02	45.88	7.65	38.23
20/4	2116	T Harrison	H04	24.96	4.16	20.80
28/4	2117	Rolls Ltd	R01	37.25	6.21	31.04
				143.19	23.87	119.32

Main ledger accounts

Sales ledger control account

£	£

Sales returns

£	£

VAT account

£	£

Subsidiary ledger accounts

Gerard & Co   G01

£	£

Filmer Ltd   F02

£	£

T Harrison   H04

£	£

Rolls Ltd   R01

£	£

32 PURCHASES RETURNS DAY BOOK

Given below is a purchases returns day book.

You are required to post the totals to the main/general ledger accounts and post the individual entries to the subsidiary ledger accounts.

Purchases returns day book						
Date	Credit note	Code	Supplier	Total £	VAT £	Purchase Returns £
15/4/X1	C0179	PL16	J D Withers	28.08	4.68	23.40
18/4/X1	C4772	PL06	F Williams	168.00	28.00	140.00
19/4/X1	06638	PL13	K Bartlett	54.24	9.04	45.20
				250.32	41.72	208.60

Main ledger

Purchases ledger control account

	£			£
		12/4	Balance b/d	12,678.57

VAT account

	£			£
		12/4	Balance b/d	1,023.90

Purchases returns account

	£			£
		12/4	Balance b/d	1,818.43

Subsidiary ledger

F Williams — PL06

	£			£
		12/4	Balance b/d	673.47

K Bartlett — PL13

	£			£
		12/4	Balance b/d	421.36

J D Withers — PL16

	£			£
		12/4	Balance b/d	446.37

33 COMBINED PURCHASES AND PURCHASE RETURNS DAY BOOK

Given below is the combined purchases and purchase returns day book for a business for the week ending 12 March 20X1.

Prepare the journal entry for the posting of the totals to the main ledger (the last journal number was 0253) and post the individual entries to the subsidiary ledger accounts given.

Purchases day book							
Date	Invoice no	Code	Supplier	Total £	VAT £	Purchases £	Purchase Returns £
08/3/X1	06121	PL12	Homer Ltd	228.64	38.11	190.53	
	11675	PL07	Forker & Co	211.66	35.28	176.38	
09/3/X1	46251	PL08	Print Co	234.94	39.16	195.78	
10/3/X1	016127	PL02	ABG Ltd	298.81	49.80	249.01	
	C4366	PL07	Forker & Co	(24.24)	(4.04)		(20.20)
11/3/X1	77918	PL19	G Greg	173.30	28.88	144.42	
	06132	PL12	Homer Ltd	193.37	32.23	161.14	
12/3/X1	CN477	PL02	ABG Ltd	(49.34)	(8.22)		(41.12)
				1,267.14	211.20	1,117.26	(61.32)

JOURNAL ENTRY	No:
Prepared by:	
Authorised by:	
Date:	
Narrative:	

Account	Debit	Credit
TOTALS		

Subsidiary ledger

		ABG Ltd		PL02
	£			£
		5/3	Balance b/d	486.90

		Forker & Co		PL07
	£			£
		5/3	Balance b/d	503.78

		Print Co		PL08
	£			£
		5/3	Balance b/d	229.56

		Homer Ltd		PL12
	£			£
		5/3	Balance b/d	734.90

		G Greg		PL19
	£			£
		5/3	Balance b/d	67.89

LEVEL I: CERTIFICATE IN BASIC BOOKKEEPING

MAKING AND RECEIVING PAYMENTS

34 CREDIT SIDE OF THE CASH BOOK

(a) The following transactions all took place on 31 July and have been entered in the credit side of the cash-book as shown below. No entries have yet been made in the ledgers.

Cash-book – Credit side

Date 20XX	Details	VAT £	Bank £
31 July	Stationery	16	96
31 July	Photocopier repair	40	240

What will be the FOUR entries in the general ledger?

General ledger

Account name	Amount £	Debit ✓	Credit ✓

The following transactions all took place on 31 July and have been entered in the debit side of the cash-book as shown below. No entries have yet been made in the ledgers.

Cash-book – Debit side

Date 20XX	Details	Discount	Bank £
31 July	Balance b/f		6,350
31 July	BBG Ltd	180	7,200
31 July	EFG Ltd		5,000

(b) **What will be the THREE entries in the sales ledger?**

Sales ledger

Account name	Amount £	Debit ✓	Credit ✓

(c) What will be the THREE entries in the general ledger?

General ledger

Account name	Amount £	Debit ✓	Credit ✓

35 ABC LTD

There are five payments to be entered in ABC Ltd's cash-book.

Receipts

| Received cash with thanks for goods bought by ABC Ltd, a customer without a credit account.

Net £180
VAT £36
Total £216

S. Lampard | Received cash with thanks for goods bought by ABC Ltd, a customer without a credit account.

Net £220
VAT £44
Total £264

S Bobbins | Received cash with thanks for goods bought by ABC Ltd, a customer without a credit account.

Net £530
(No VAT)

Penny Rhodes |

Cheque book counterfoils

| Henley's Ltd
(Purchase ledger account HEN002)

£4,925
(Note: Have taken £125 settlement discount)

000372 | Epic Equipment Maintenance
(We have no credit account with this supplier)

£480 incl VAT

000373 |

(a) Enter the details from the three receipts and two cheque book stubs into the credit side of the cash-book shown below and total each column.

Cash-book – credit side

Details	Discount	Cash	Bank	VAT	Creditors	Cash purchases	Repairs and Renewals
Balance b/f							
S. Lampard							
S. Bobbins							
Penny Rhodes							
Henley's Ltd							
Epic Equipment Maintenance							
Total							

There are two cheques from credit customers to be entered in ABC Ltd's cash book:

D. Davies £851

E. Denholm £450 (this customer has taken a £25 discount)

(b) Enter the above details into the debit side of the cash-book and total each column.

Cash book – debit side

Details	Discount	Cash	Bank	Receivables
Balance b/f		1,550	7,425	
D Davies				
E Denholm				
Total				

(c) Using your answers to (a) and (b) above calculate the cash balance.

£ ☐

(d) Using your answers to (a) and (b) above calculate the bank balance.

£ ☐

(e) Will the bank balance calculated in (d) above be a debit or credit balance?

Debit / Credit

PRACTICE QUESTIONS: SECTION 1

36 CHEQUES FROM DEBTORS

Your organisation receives a number of cheques from debtors through the post each day and these are listed on the cheque listing. It also makes some cash sales each day which include VAT at the standard rate.

Today's date is 28 April 20X1 and the cash sales today were £265.08. The cheque listing for the day is given below:

Cheque listing 28 April 20X1

G Heilbron	£108.45
L Tessa	£110.57 – settlement discount of £3.31 taken
J Dent	£210.98 – settlement discount of £6.32 taken
F Trainer	£97.60
A Winter	£105.60 – settlement discount of £3.16 taken

An extract from the customer file shows the following:

Customer	Sales ledger code
J Dent	SL17
G Heilbron	SL04
L Tessa	SL15
F Trainer	SL21
A Winter	SL09

Required:

(a) Write up the cash receipts book given below and total each of the columns.

(b) Post the totals of the cash receipts book to the main/general ledger accounts.

(c) Post the individual receipts to the subsidiary ledger (the sales ledger).

Cash receipts book

Date	Narrative	SL Code	Total	VAT	SLCA	Cash sales	Discount
			£	£	£	£	£

Main ledger

VAT account

£	£

Sales ledger control account

£	£

Sales account

£	£

Discount allowed account

£	£

Subsidiary ledger

G Heilbron — SL04

£	£

L Tessa — SL15

£	£

J Dent — SL17

£	£

F Trainer — SL21

£	£

A Winter — SL09

£	£

PRACTICE QUESTIONS: SECTION 1

37 CHEQUE LISTING FOR YOUR ORGANISATION

Given below is the cheque listing for your organisation showing all of the cheques received in the week ending 15 May 20X1.

Customer	Sales ledger code	£	Discount taken £
McCaul & Partners	M04	147.56	2.95
Dunn Associates	D02	264.08	
P Martin	M02	167.45	
F Little	L03	265.89	7.97
D Raine	R01	158.02	3.95

There were also cash sales of £446.50 including standard rate VAT during the week.

Required:

(a) Write up the cash receipts book given below and total each of the columns.

(b) Post the totals to the main/general ledger accounts.

(c) Post the individual receipts to the subsidiary ledger accounts (the sales ledger).

Cash receipts book

Date	Narrative	SL Code	Total	VAT	SLCA	Cash sales	Discount
			£	£	£	£	£

Main ledger

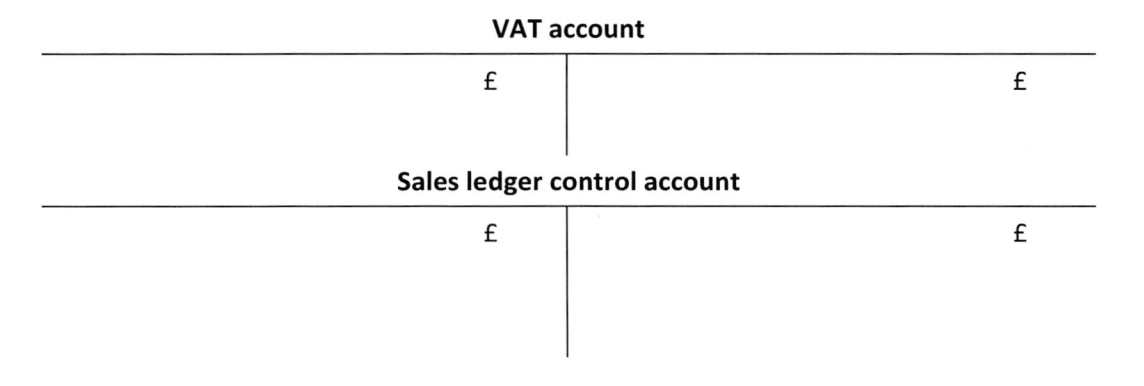

VAT account

£	£

Sales ledger control account

£	£

Sales account

£	£

Discount allowed

£	£

Subsidiary ledger

McCaul & Partners

£	£

Dunn Associates

£	£

P Martin

£	£

F Little

£	£

D Raine

£	£

38 CHEQUE LISTING FOR A BUSINESS

Given below is the cheque listing for a business for the week ending 12 March 20X1.

Cheque payment listing

Supplier	Code	Cheque number	Cheque amount £	Discount taken £
Homer Ltd	PL12	03648	168.70	5.06
Forker & Co	PL07	03649	179.45	5.38
Cash purchases		03650	334.87	
Print Associates	PL08	03651	190.45	
ABG Ltd	PL02	03652	220.67	6.62
Cash purchases		03653	193.87	
G Greg	PL19	03654	67.89	

Required:

(a) enter the payments into the cash payments book and total each of the columns;

(b) post the totals to the main/general ledger accounts given;

(c) post the individual entries to the subsidiary ledger accounts given.

Cash payments book

Date	Narrative	PL Code	Total £	VAT £	PLCA £	Cash purchases £	Discounts £

Main ledger

Purchases ledger control account

		£			£
			5/3	Balance b/d	4,136.24

VAT account

		£			£
			5/3	Balance b/d	1,372.56

Purchases account

		£			£
5/3	Balance b/d	20,465.88			

Discounts received account

		£			£
			5/3	Balance b/d	784.56

Subsidiary ledger

ABG Ltd   PL02

		£			£
			5/3	Balance b/d	486.90

Forker & Co   PL07

		£			£
			5/3	Balance b/d	503.78

Print Associates   PL08

		£			£
			5/3	Balance b/d	229.56

	Homer Ltd			PL12
£				£
	5/3	Balance b/d		734.90

	G Greg			PL19
£				£
	5/3	Balance b/d		67.89

39 CHEQUE PAYMENT

Given below is the cheque payment listing for a business for the week ending 8 May 20X1.

Cheque payment listing

Supplier	Code	Cheque number	Cheque amount £	Discount taken £
G Rails	PL04	001221	177.56	4.43
L Jameson	PL03	001222	257.68	7.73
Cash purchases		001223	216.43	
K Davison	PL07	001224	167.89	
T Ives	PL01	001225	289.06	5.79
Cash purchases		001226	263.78	
H Samuels	PL02	001227	124.36	

The cash purchases include VAT at the standard rate.

Required:

(a) enter the payments into the cash payments book and total each of the columns;

(b) complete the journal for the posting of the totals to the main/general ledger – the last journal entry was number 1467;

(c) post the individual entries to the subsidiary ledger accounts given.

Cash payments book

Date	Narrative	PL Code	Total £	VAT £	Creditors £	Cash purchases £	Discounts £

JOURNAL ENTRY	No:	
Prepared by:		
Authorised by:		
Date:		
Narrative:		
Account	Debit	Credit
TOTALS		

Subsidiary ledger

T Ives — PL01

	£			£
		1 May	Balance b/d	332.56

H Samuels — PL02

	£			£
		1 May	Balance b/d	286.90

L Jameson — PL03

	£			£
		1 May	Balance b/d	623.89

G Rails — PL04

	£			£
		1 May	Balance b/d	181.99

K Davison — PL07

	£			£
		1 May	Balance b/d	167.89

40 PAPERBOX LTD

Today is 19 February 20X0. You are the cashier at Paperbox Ltd.

You are required to complete the following tasks.

Task 1 Using the remittance lists prepare the paying in slip and credit card voucher summary for paying these amounts in to the bank.

Task 2 Write up the cash book for monies included on the paying in slip.

Mail order sales are recorded on the remittance list including VAT.

Task 3 Prepare a journal entry to post the **totals** from the cash receipts book to the accounts in the general ledger.

The last journal entry was number 105.

REMITTANCE LIST

Date: 19 - 2 - X0
Receipts from: **TRADE DEBTORS**

Customer name	Invoice No	Cheque £	Credit Card Express £	Credit Card Global £	Discount £
NJ Peal	5229, 5248	291.60			
Stationery Supplies	5392	245.30			5.01
Candle Company Ltd	5227, 5309	562.80			4.95
Pearce & Fellows	5308	659.18			13.45
Abraham Matthews Ltd	5291	117.93			
Total		1,876.81			23.41

REMITTANCE LIST

Date: 19 - 2 - X0
Receipts from: Mail Order

Customer name	Invoice No	Cheque £	Credit Card Express £	Credit Card Global £	Discount £
KB Smith			22.60		
R Jones			5.83		
C Bastok			26.18		
J Rirolli			18.95		
Total			73.56		

REMITTANCE LIST

Date: 19 - 2 - X0
Receipts from: Sundry

Customer name	Invoice No	Cheque £	Credit Card Express £	Credit Card Global £	Discount £
RF Wholesalers Ltd	Rent	539.50			
(Not trade debtor)					
(Exempt from VAT)					
Total		539.50			

Bank paying-in slip

		To be retained by receiving bank			
For the credit of _____						
Cheques etc for collection to be included in total credit of £ _____ paid in _____ 20__.						
	£	brought forward	£	brought forward	£
Carried forward	£	carried forward	£	Total cheques etc	£

Date _____

Cashier's stamp and initials

56 – 28 – 48

FINANCIAL BANK PLC

GREENOCK

£50 Notes	
£20 Notes	
£10 Notes	
£5 Notes	
£2 Coins	
£1 Coins	
50p	
20p	
Silver	
Bronze	
Total Cash	
Cheques, POs etc	
TOTAL £	

Fee | No Chqs | Paid in by _____

Address/Ref No. _____

Credit card voucher summary

Please do not pin or staple this voucher as this will affect the machine processing.

All sales vouchers must be deposited within three banking days of the dates shown on them.

If you are submitting more than 26 vouchers please enclose a separate listing.

If a voucher contravenes the terms of the retailer agreement then the amount shown on the voucher may be charged back to your bank account, either direct or via your paying in branch.

Similarly, if the total amount shown on the Retail Voucher Summary does not balance with our total of vouchers, the difference will be credited (or debited) to your bank account.

	£	p
1		
2		
3		
4		
5		
6		
7		
8		
9		
10		
11		
12		
13		
14		
15		
16		
17		
18		
19		
20		
21		

SALES VOUCHERS   TOTAL

Cash Book Receipts

Date	Narrative	Total	SLCA	Mail Order Sales	Other	VAT	Discount allowed

Journal no. _____
Date _____
Prepared by _____

Code	Account	Debit	Credit
601	Cash at bank (deposit)		
102	Sales mail order		
202	Bank interest		
504	Trade debtors		
605	VAT control account		
409	Discounts allowed		
504	Trade debtors		
Total			

Narrative

THE TRIAL BALANCE

41 SMITH & SON

Below is a list of balances to be transferred to the trial balance of Smith & Son at 31 Dec.

Place the figures in the debit or credit column, as appropriate, and total each column.

Account name	Amount £	Debit £	Credit £
Fixtures and Fittings	8,250		
Capital	18,400		
Bank overdraft	4,870		
Petty cash control	350		
Sales ledger control	42,870		
Purchases ledger control	23,865		
VAT owed to tax authorities	10,245		
Stock	9,870		
Loan from bank	22,484		
Sales	180,264		
Sales returns	5,420		
Purchases	129,030		
Purchases returns	2,678		
Discount allowed	2,222		
Discount received	3,432		
Heat and Light	1,490		
Motor expenses	2,354		
Wages	42,709		
Rent and rates	10,600		
Repairs	3,020		
Hotel expenses	1,890		
Telephone	2,220		
Delivery costs	1,276		
Miscellaneous expenses	2,667		
Totals			

42 EXPIALIDOCIOUS LTD

Below is a list of balances to be transferred to the trial balance of Expialidocious Ltd as at 31 July.

Place the figures in the debit or credit column, as appropriate, and total each column.

Account name	Amount £	Debit £	Credit £
Capital	25,360		
Petty cash control	250		
Loan from bank	11,600		
Sales ledger control	159,242		
Purchases ledger control	83,682		
Motor vehicles	35,900		
Stock	28,460		
Bank overdraft	10,063		
Owed from tax authorities	15,980		
Purchases	343,014		
Purchases returns	1,515		
Wages	56,150		
Motor expenses	2,950		
Interest income	400		
Sales	532,900		
Sales returns	5,760		
Stationery	1,900		
Light & heat	6,500		
Discount received	200		
Discount allowed	2,160		
Interest paid on overdraft	550		
Travel	1,800		
Marketing	650		
Telephone	1,510		
Miscellaneous expenses	2,944		
Totals			

43 RICK'S RACERS

	Balances extracted on 30 June £	Balances at 1 July Debit £	Balances at 1 July Credit £
Motor vehicles	24,200	24,200	
Plant and Equipment	22,350	22,350	
Stock	9,000	9,000	
Cash at Bank	11,217	11,217	
Cash	150	150	
Sales ledger control	131,275	131,275	
Purchases ledger control	75,336		75,336
VAT owing to tax authorities	15,127		15,127
Capital	14,417		26,247
Bank Loan	12,500		12,500
Sales	276,132		276,132
Purchases	152,476	152,476	
Wages	35,465	35,465	
Motor expenses	3,617	3,617	
Repairs and Renewals	2,103	2,103	
Rent and rates	3,283	3,283	
Light and Heat	4,012	4,012	
Insurance	4,874	4,874	
Sundry Expenses	1,230	1,320	
Suspense account (credit balance)	11,740	—	—
Totals		405,342	405,342

44 CB INTERIOR'S

CB Interiors' initial trial balance includes a suspense account with a balance of £8,640 The error has been traced to the purchase day-book shown below.

Purchase day-book

Date 20XX	Details	Invoice number	Total £	VAT £	Net £
30 Jun	Able Paints Ltd	2,763	2,400	400	2,000
30 Jun	Matley Materials	2,764	3,120	520	2,600
30 Jun	Teesdale Parts	2,765	4,080	680	3,400
	Totals		960	1,600	8,000

(a) Identify the error and record the journal entry needed in the general ledger to correct it and remove the suspense account.

Account name	Amount £	Debit ✓	Credit ✓

(b) An entry to record a bank payment of £750 for repairs has been reversed.

Record the journal entries needed in the general ledger to

(i) remove the incorrect entry.

(ii) record the correct entry.

Account name	Amount £	Debit ✓	Credit ✓

45 JUNIPER JUNGLE'S

Juniper Jungle's trial balance was extracted and did not balance. The debit column of the trial balance totalled £442,735 and the credit column totalled £428,372

(a) What entry would be made in the suspense account to balance the trial balance.

Account name	Amount £	Debit ✓	Credit ✓
Suspense			

(b) Show which of the errors below are, or are not, disclosed by the trial balance.

Error in the general ledger	Error disclosed by the trial balance	Error NOT disclosed by the trial balance
Incorrectly calculating the balance on the Motor Vehicles account		
Recording a receipt for commission received in the bank interest received account		
Recording a bank receipt for bank interest received on the debit side of both the bank account and the bank interest received account		
Recording supplier invoices on the debit side of the purchase ledger control account and the credit side of the purchases account		
Recording a payment by cheque to a payable in the purchase ledger control account only		
Recording a bank payment of £124 for insurance as £142 in the insurance account and £124 in the bank account		

46 TRIAL BALANCE

Given below are the balances of a business at 31 May 20X1.

	£
Purchases	385,800
Creditors	32,000
Computer	8,000
Motor car	19,200
Discount received	3,850
Telephone	4,320
Sales returns	6,720
Wages	141,440
VAT (credit balance)	7,200
Drawings	60,000
Discount allowed	6,400
Rent and rates	26,200
Debtors	53,500
Motor expenses	7,700
Sales	642,080
Stock	38,880
Inland Revenue	3,800
Purchases returns	2,560
Electricity	6,080
Bank (debit balance)	1,920
Capital	74,670

Required:

Prepare the trial balance as at 31 May 20X1.

PRACTICE QUESTIONS: **SECTION 1**

47 LEDGER ACCOUNTS

Given below are the ledger accounts for the first month of trading for a small business.

Capital account

					£
			1 Mar	Bank	12,000

Bank account

		£			£
1 Mar	Capital	12,000	2 Mar	Motor car	4,500
7 Mar	Sales	3,000	2 Mar	Purchases	2,400
20 Mar	Sales	2,100	14 Mar	Rent	600
26 Mar	Debtors	3,800	18 Mar	Stationery	200
			25 Mar	Creditors	3,100
			28 Mar	Drawings	1,600

Motor car account

		£			£
2 Mar	Bank	4,500			

Purchases account

		£			£
2 Mar	Bank	2,400			
4 Mar	Creditors	2,500			
12 Mar	Creditors	4,100			

Purchase ledger control account

		£			£
25 Mar	Bank	3,100	4 Mar	Purchases	2,500
			12 Mar	Purchases	4,100

KAPLAN PUBLISHING

Sales account

		£			£
			7 Mar	Bank	3,000
			10 Mar	Debtors	4,600
			15 Mar	Debtors	3,500
			20 Mar	Bank	2,100

Sales ledger control account

		£			£
10 Mar	Sales	4,600	26 Mar	Bank	3,800
15 Mar	Sales	3,500			

Rent account

		£			£
14 Mar	Bank	600			

Stationery account

		£			£
18 Mar	Bank	200			

Drawings account

		£			£
28 Mar	Bank	1,600			

Required:

Balance off the ledger accounts and produce a trial balance at the end of the first month of trading.

UNDERPINNING KNOWLEDGE

48 PURCHASES

When a company purchases a new stapler so that accounts clerks can staple together relevant pieces of paper, the amount of the purchase is debited to the fittings and equipment (cost) account.

(a) Is this treatment correct?

(b) If so, why; if not, why not?

49 ENGINE REPAIR

If one of a company's vans had to have its engine repaired at a cost of £1,800, would this represent capital or revenue expenditure? Give brief reasons.

50 ACCOUNTING EQUATION

Financial accounting is based upon the accounting equation.

(a) Show whether the following statements are true or false.

Assets less capital are equal to liabilities	True False
Assets plus liabilities are equal to capital	True False
Capital plus liabilities are equal to assets	True False

(b) Classify each of the following items as an asset or a liability by using the drop down lists.

Item	Asset	Liability
	✔	✔
Stock		
Machinery		
5 year loan		
Vehicle used by a business		
VAT owed to the tax authorities		
Debtors		
Creditors		

LEVEL I: CERTIFICATE IN BASIC BOOKKEEPING

51 CAPITAL VS. REVENUE

Select one option in each instance below to show whether the item will be capital income, revenue income, capital expenditure or revenue expenditure.

Item	Capital income	Revenue income	Capital expenditure	Revenue expenditure
Receipt from sale of motor vehicle				
Purchase of machinery				
Payment of electricity bill				
Purchase of goods for resale				
Receipts from cash sales				
Receipts from debtors				
Payments of salaries to staff				

52 BLOSSOM BLOOMS

Blossom Blooms receives payment from customers and makes payments to suppliers in a variety of ways.

(a) Select FOUR checks that DO NOT have to be made on each of the two payment methods shown below when received from customers.

Checks to be made	Cheque	Telephone credit card payment
Check expiry date		
Check issue number		
Check not post-dated		
Check security number		
Check words and figures match		
Check card has not been tampered with		

(b) Show whether each of the statements below is true or false.

When Blossom Blooms makes payments to suppliers by debit card, the amount paid affects the bank current account

True / False

When Blossom Blooms makes payments to suppliers by credit card, the amount paid affects the bank current account

True / False

53
The types of documentation that might accompany a complex transaction for a piece of machinery include three of the following. Which is the odd one out?

A   Invoice for outstanding amount from manufacturer

B   Initial enquiry letter from manufacturer

C   Price quotation for machinery from manufacturer

D   Deposit remittance from purchaser

54
Which of the following does not contain an amount in money?

A   Delivery note

B   Quotation

C   Payslip

D   Receipt

55
Which of the following lists is in the correct chronological order?

A   Sign petty cash voucher, spend money, obtain receipt, authorise voucher

B   Quotation, purchase order, purchase invoice, cheque requisition

C   Invoice, credit note, debit note, delivery note, remittance advice

D   Receipt, purchase invoice, statement, despatch note

56
Which document is used by a supplier to correct an earlier overcharge?

A   Advice note

B   Credit note

C   Debit note

D   Invoice

57
From the following list of situations where an invoice has been sent, choose one that would not require a credit note to be raised:

A   A customer has returned some or all of the goods because they are damaged or faulty

B   A customer has returned some or all of the goods because they are not the ones that were ordered

C   A customer has never received the goods although an invoice was sent out

D   Postage and packaging was omitted on the original invoice

58 Which of the following describes a goods received note?

    A   It is a formal request, sent by a business to a supplier requesting the delivery of the goods specified on the purchase order

    B   It is an internal check document that serves as a record of the quantity and condition of goods that have been delivered to the business

    C   It is a discount that is offered to a customer if the invoice is paid by a certain date

    D   It is a means of identifying a transaction as being of a particular type by allocating to it an appropriate reference number

59 Which of the following documents would not be entered in the accounting records after it has been raised?

    A   A credit note

    B   A debit note

    C   A quotation

    D   A payslip

60 LEGAL POSITION

You are working in the accounts office of your company and get a telephone call from someone who says that he is the bank manager of North Bank in the High Street. He has been approached by Mr Donald Snow, a customer of your company, for a loan to pay off the debt he still owes you. He asks how much Mr Snow owes, and he would also like to check whether, according to your records, Mr Snow is married or divorced.

What is the legal position?

61 What is the bank clearing system?

    A   Agreeing a loan or overdraft between bank and customer

    B   The transfer of cheques between the payee's bank to payment at the drawer's bank

    C   The electronic transfer of funds enabling a supplier to be instantly paid by debit card

    D   Checking customer references before they are given a credit card

62 Which is unique to a bank customer?

    A   Account number

    B   Cheque number

    C   Drawee

    D   Sort code

63 John makes a regular monthly payment from his bank account to his daughter's bank account to cover her living expenses while she is at university.

What method of payment is John using?

    A   'Account payee' crossed cheque

    B   BACS

    C   Direct debit

    D   Standing order

64 A bank dishonours a cheque on a partnership account because there are insufficient funds on the account. Who must now pay the outstanding amount?

    A   The bank

    B   The partnership

    C   The payee of the cheque

    D   The person who was the authorised signatory

65 When banking cash, general security procedures should be followed wherever possible. Which of the following is the most risky?

    A   Ensuring that the employee taking the cash to the bank or night safe is accompanied by another employee

    B   Going to the bank or the night safe at different times of day or by a different route

    C   Using the same responsible employee to take the cash to the bank

    D   Using a security firm to transport the cash to the bank if necessary

66 Suppose that the following cheques need signing as soon as possible:

	Cheque No.	Amount
		£
(a)	11723	5,379.20
(b)	11724	1,406.29
(c)	11725	293.50
(d)	11726	20,501.80

Given below are the authorised cheque signatories:

G Gammage	Finance Director
F Freud	Managing Director
P Palim	Marketing Director
T Timms	Finance Manager
S Simon	Production Manager

The cheque signatory limits are:

Amounts up to £1,000	One manager
£1,001 to £2,000	Two managers
£2,001 to £5,000	One director
£5,001 to £10,000	Two directors
£10,001 to £20,000	One director plus the finance director
Over £20,000	Managing director plus the finance director

Who can sign each of these cheques?

67 When may a bank return a cheque to the payee?

(i) When it is more than six month out of date.

(ii) When it is unsigned.

(iii) When the account holder has insufficient funds to cover the cheque.

(iv) When the cheque is crossed 'A/c payee' and it is presented by the named payee.

A (i), (ii) and (iii)

B (i), (ii) and (iv)

C (i), (iii) and (iv)

D (ii), (iii) and (iv)

68 In relation to the law of contract, define and explain consideration.

69 In relation to contract law explain the meaning and effect of:

(a) an offer

(b) an invitation to treat.

70 An advertisement to sell a car in a newspaper will amount to

- A   An offer
- B   A mere statement of price
- C   An invitation to treat
- D   A declaration of intent

71 An offer was made by letter posted in London and delivered in Birmingham. A reply was made by fax machine in Manchester and received by the offeror's fax machine in Liverpool.

Where was the contract made?

- A   Where the offer was made in London
- B   Where the acceptance was put into the fax machine in Manchester
- C   Where the acceptance was received on the fax machine in Liverpool
- D   Where the letter making the offer was received in Birmingham

72 In relation to social and domestic agreements the court

- A   Assumes the parties did intend to create a legally binding contract
- B   Presumes that the parties did not intend to create a legally binding contract
- C   Does not consider the intention of the parties
- D   Does not make any presumptions about the intention of the parties

73 S offers to sell his car to B for £10,000 cash. At what point in time does the contract come into being?

- A   When B accepts the offer
- B   When B pays S the £10,000
- C   When the agreement is written down
- D   When the agreement is signed

74 A plc has been induced to enter into a contract by the fraudulent misrepresentation of B. Which of the following is *incorrect*?

- A   A plc may be able to rescind the contract
- B   A plc may be able to claim damages and then rescind the contract
- C   A plc is entitled to rescind the contract and to claim the damages
- D   A plc is entitled to refuse to perform the contract if it is still executory

75 Frustration discharges a contract when

- A A contract is impossible to perform at the time it is made
- B An event occurs after the contract has been made rendering the performance more difficult and expensive to perform
- C An event occurs after the contract has been made rendering its performance impossible
- D A party expressly promises to do something which he later decided is not in his best interests

76 Rosemary offered by letter to sell Mary her motorbike for £5,000. Mary wrote back saying she accepted the offer and would pay in two instalments at the end of the two following months. Is there a contract?

- A No, because Mary is trying to amend the contractual terms, Rosemary can be assumed to revoke the offer
- B Yes, there has been an offer and acceptance and a binding contract applies
- C No, Mary's response constitutes a counter-offer and is effectively a rejection of Rosemary's offer
- D Yes, Mary's response is merely a clarification of contractual terms

77 Which of the following rules regarding consideration is *incorrect*?

- A Every simple contract must be supported by consideration
- B Consideration must move from the promisee
- C Consideration must be adequate
- D Consideration must be sufficient

Section 2

PRACTICE ANSWERS

BUSINESS DOCUMENTS

1 NAN NURSING

Has the correct purchase price of the chocolate puddings been charged?	**N**
Has the correct discount been calculated?	**Y**
What would be the VAT amount charged if the invoice was correct?	**£18.00**
What would be the total amount charged if the invoice was correct?	**£108.00**

2 ALESSANDRO LTD

(a) **Invoice**

Alessandro Ltd
8 Alan Street
Glasgow, G1 7DJ
VAT Registration No. 398 2774 01

Palermo Wholesale
17 Zoo Lane
Dartford
DH8 4TJ

Customer account code: AGG42

Delivery note number: 24369
Date: 1 Aug 20XX

Invoice No: 327

Quantity	Product code	Total list price £	Net amount after discount £	VAT £	Gross £
40	SB05	2,500	2,200	418.00	2,618

(b)

Settlement discount

KAPLAN PUBLISHING

LEVEL I: CERTIFICATE IN BASIC BOOKKEEPING

3 ALPHA LTD

Has the correct product been supplied by Pixie Paper? Y

Has the correct net price been calculated? ***N**

Is the total invoice price correct? **N**

What would be the VAT amount charged if the invoice was correct? **£90**

What would be the total amount charged if the invoice was correct? **£540**

* the trade discount of 10% should have been deducted so that the net price was £450. VAT @ 20% on the net price of £450 is then calculated as £90.

4 ABG LTD

(a) Purchase return £900

(b) Invoice 486

(c) £8,580

5 KEYBOARD SUPPLIES

CREDIT NOTE

Credit Note to:
H M Music
Tenant House
Perley TN7 8ER

Keyboard Supplies
Trench Park Estate
Fieldham
Sussex TN21 4AF
Tel: 01829 654545
Fax: 01829 654646

Credit Note no: CN0337
Tax point: 17 April 20X1
VAT reg no: 466 1128 30
Your reference: SL09
Purchase order no:

Code	Description	Quantity	VAT rate %	Unit price £	Amount exclusive of VAT £
B3060	Bento Keyboard	1	20	126.00	126.00

	126.00
Trade discount 15%	18.90
	107.10
VAT at 20%	21.42
Total amount	128.52

6 ELECTRONIC KEYBOARDS

INVOICE

Invoice to:
Musicolor Ltd
23 High Street
Nutford
Sussex TN11 4TZ

Keyboard Supplies
Trench Park Estate
Fieldham
Sussex TN21 4AF
Tel: 01829 654545
Fax: 01829 654646

Deliver to:

As above

Invoice no:	06113
Tax point:	17 April 20X1
VAT reg no:	466 1128 30
Your reference:	SL06
Purchase order no:	04 318

Code	Description	Quantity	VAT rate %	Unit price £	Amount exclusive of VAT £
Z4600	Zanni Keyboard	2	20	185.00	370.00
A4802	Atol Keyboard	3	20	130.00	390.00

	760.00
Trade discount 10%	76.00
	684.00
VAT at 20%	132.69
Total amount payable	816.69

Deduct discount of 3% if paid within 10 days, 30 days net

7 FARMHOUSE PICKLES LTD

				Farmhouse Pickles Ltd
				225 School Lane
				Weymouth
				Dorset
				WE36 5NR
			Tel:	0261 480444
			Fax:	0261 480555
To:	Grant & Co		Date:	

STATEMENT

Date	Transaction	Debit £	Credit £	Balance £
1 April	Opening balance			337.69
4 April	Inv 32656	150.58		488.27
12 April	Credit 0335		38.70	449.57
18 April	Inv 32671	179.52		629.09
20 April	Payment		330.94	
	Discount		6.75	291.40
24 April	Credit 0346		17.65	273.75
25 April	Inv 32689	94.36		368.11

May we remind you that our credit terms are 30 days

				Farmhouse Pickles Ltd
				225 School Lane
				Weymouth
				Dorset
				WE36 5NR
			Tel:	0261 480444
			Fax:	0261 480555
To:	Mitchell Partners		Date:	

STATEMENT

Date	Transaction	Debit £	Credit £	Balance £
1 April	Opening balance			180.46
7 April	Inv 32662	441.57		622.03
12 April	Credit 0344		66.89	555.14
20 April	Inv 32669	274.57		829.71
21 April	Payment		613.58	
	Discount		8.45	207.68

May we remind you that our credit terms are 30 days

8 NETHAN BUILDERS

Discrepancies:

1 The wrong quantity of PL432115 was delivered to the customer (they ordered 15 and 14 were delivered).

2 The unit costs are incorrect on the invoice: they have been switched around.

3 The VAT has been calculated without taking into account the settlement discount.

PRACTICE ANSWERS: **SECTION 2**

BOOKS OF ORIGINAL ENTRY

9   (a)   £140.00 × 20%   =   £28.00

       (b)   £560.00 × 20%   =   £112.00

       (c)   £780.00 × $\dfrac{20}{120}$ =   £130.00

       (d)   £970.00 × $\dfrac{20}{120}$ =   £161.66

10   (a)   £(280 − (2% × 280)) × 20%   =   £54.88

       (b)   £(480 − (3% × 480)) × 20%   =   £93.12

       (c)   £(800 − (5% × 800)) × 20%   =   £152.00

       (d)   £(650 − (4% × 650)) × 20%   =   £124.80

11   **ARISTOTLE**

       (a)   **Bairstow takes the settlement discount:**

	£
Net price	600.00
VAT £(600 − (3% × 600)) × 20%	116.40
Invoice value	716.40

Amount paid by B:

	£
Invoice value	716.40
Less: 3% × 600	(18.00)
Amount paid	698.40

       (b)   **Bairstow does not take the settlement discount:**

If Bairstow does not take the settlement discount they will pay the full invoice value of £716.40.

12 AARDVARK

(a) **Christie takes the settlement discount:**

	£
Net price	700.00
VAT £(700 − (5% × 700)) × 20%	133.00
Invoice value	833.00
Less: 5% discount = 700 × 5%	(35.00)
	798.00

Total sale value to be entered into general ledger: **£700**

Total to be paid be Christie: **£798**

(b) **Christie does not take the settlement discount:**

Total sale value to be entered into general ledger: **£700**

Total to be paid be Christie: **£833**

13 SALES DAY BOOK

Sales day-book

Date 20XX	Details	Invoice number	Total £	VAT £	Net £	Sales type 1 £	Sales type 2 £
31 Dec	Poonams	105	3,600	600	3,000		3,000
31 Dec	D Taylor	106	7,680	1,280	6,400	6,400	
31 Dec	Smiths	107	3,840	640	3,200		3,200
	Totals		15,120	2,520	12,600	6,400	6,200

14 LADY LTD

General ledger

Purchases ledger control account

	£		£
		1 Dec Balance b/d	5,103.90
		18 Dec Purchases & VAT	**903.23**

VAT account

	£		£
		1 Dec Balance b/d	526.90
18 Dec PLCA	**150.53**		

Purchases account

	£		£
1 Dec Balance b/d	22,379.52		
18 Dec PLCA	**752.70**		

Subsidiary Ledger

M Brown

	£		£
		1 Dec Balance b/d	68.50
		1 Dec PDB	**300.00**

H Madden

	£		£
		1 Dec Balance b/d	286.97
		5 Dec PDB	**183.55**

L Singh

	£		£
		1 Dec Balance b/d	125.89
		7 Dec PDB	**132.60**

A Stevens

	£		£
		1 Dec Balance b/d	12.36
		10 Dec PDB	**90.00**

N Shema

	£		£
		1 Dec Balance b/d	168.70
		18 Dec PDB	**197.08**

15 BUTTONS LTD

(a) **What will be the entries in the purchases ledger?**

Account name	Amount £	Debit ✓	Credit ✓
Peak & Co	6,240		✓
Max Ltd	12,720		✓
McIntyre Wholesale	5,760		✓
Pigmy Ltd	3,744		✓

(b) **What will be the entries in the general ledger?**

Account name	Amount £	Debit ✓	Credit ✓
Purchases	23,720	✓	
VAT	4,744	✓	
Purchase ledger control	28,464		✓

16 FREDDIE LTD

Purchases day-book

Date 20XX	Details	Invoice number	Total £	VAT £	Net £	Product 14211 £	Product 14212 £
31 July	Box Ltd	SI063	960	160	800	800	
31 July	Shrew Ltd	367FL	14,400	2,400	12,000	12,000	
31 July	Novot & Co	2176	4,800	800	4,000		4,000
	Totals		20,160	3,360	16,800	12,800	4,000

17 LOUIS LTD

(a) **What will be the entries in the sales ledger?**

Account name	Amount £	Debit ✓	Credit ✓
Sheep & Co	3,840	✓	
Cow Ltd	11,760	✓	
Chicken & Partners	6,720	✓	
Pig Ltd	14,496	✓	

(b) **What will be the entries in the general ledger?**

Account name	Amount £	Debit ✓	Credit ✓
Sales ledger Control	36,816	✓	
VAT	6,136		✓
Sales	30,680		✓

18 RING RING TELEPHONE'S

(a) **VAT control account**

VAT control

Details	Amount £	Details	Amount £
Sales returns (SRDB)	360	Sales (SDB)	30,600
Purchases (PDB)	16,200	Cash sales (CRB)	48
		Purchases returns (PRDB)	1,160
Balance c/d	15,248		
	31,808		31,808
		Balance b/d	15,248

(b) **No** – it is £15,248 owed **to** the tax authorities.

PRACTICE ANSWERS: SECTION 2

19 D F ENGINEERING

Sales day book

Date	Invoice No	Customer name	Code	Total £	VAT £	Net £
20X1						
1/5	03466	Fraser & Co	SL14	154.41	25.73	128.68
	03467	Letterhead Ltd	SL03	309.48	51.58	257.90
2/5	03468	Jeliteen Traders	SL15	115.89	19.31	96.58
3/5	03469	Harper Bros	SL22	321.78	53.63	268.15
	03470	Juniper Ltd	SL17	126.45	21.07	105.38
4/5	03471	H G Frank	SL30	353.60	58.93	294.67
5/5	03472	Keller Assocs	SL07	132.69	22.11	110.58
				1,514.30	252.36	1,261.94

20 KEYBOARD SUPPLIES

Sales day book

Date	Inv. No	Customer name	Code	Total £	VAT £	01 £	02 £	03 £	04 £
20X1									
18/4	06116	BZS Music	SL01	1,455.72	236.52		432.00		787.20
18/4	06117	M T Retail	SL29	642.00	107.00	210.00			325.00
18/4	06118	Harmer & Co	SL17	1,037.59	168.59		575.00	294.00	
				3,135.31	512.11	210.00	1,007.00	294.00	1,112.20

Note that when a trade discount has been deducted on the invoice in total it must be deducted from each type of sale when entering the figures in the analysed sales day book.

21 NETHAN BUILDERS PURCHASE INVOICES

Purchases day book

Date	Invoice no	Code	Supplier	Total	VAT	Wood	Bricks/cement	Consumables
3/5/X1	077401	PL16	Magnum Supplies	504.23	82.63		421.60	
	046193	PL08	A J Broom & Co Ltd	121.00	20.17	85.08		15.75
	47823	PL13	Jenson Ltd	442.74	71.94	284.80	86.00	
				1,067.97	174.74	369.88	507.60	15.75

22 NETHAN BUILDERS CREDIT NOTES

Purchases returns day book

Date	Credit note no	Code	Supplier	Total	VAT	Wood	Bricks/cement	Consumables
3/5/X1	CN06113	PL13	Jenson Ltd	30.85	5.14	25.71		
	06132	PL03	Haddow Bros	42.72	7.12	35.60		
	C4163	PL16	Magnum Supplies	46.92	7.82		39.10	
				120.49	20.08	61.31	39.10	–

PRACTICE ANSWERS: SECTION 2

LEDGER ACCOUNTS AND THE DIVISION OF THE LEDGER

23 ANNAND

Bank

	£		£
(a) Capital	5,000	(b) Purchases	800
(e) Sales	600	(c) Rent	500
(f) Sales	700	(d) Van	2,000
		(g) Purchases	1,000
		(h) Stationery	200
		(i) Drawings	500

Purchases

	£		£
(b) Bank	800		
(g) Bank	1,000		

Capital

	£		£
		(a) Bank	5,000

Rent

	£		£
(c) Bank	500		

Van

	£		£
(d) Bank	2,000		

Sales

	£		£
		(e) Bank	600
		(f) Bank	700

Stationery

	£		£
(h) Bank	200		

Drawings

	£		£
(i) Bank	500		

24 BERYL

Capital

	£		£
		(a) Bank	4,000

Purchases

	£		£
(b) Bank	700		
(g) Bank	1,200		

Entertainment

	£		£
(c) Bank	300		

Computers

	£		£
(d) Bank	3,000		

Sales

	£		£
		(e) Bank	1,500

Drawings

	£		£
(f) Bank	500		

Telephone

	£		£
(h) Bank	600	(i) Bank	200

Stationery

	£		£
(j) Bank	157		

Bank

	£		£
(a) Capital	4,000	(b) Purchases	700
(e) Sales	1,500	(c) Entertainment	300
(i) Telephone	200	(d) Computers	3,000
		(f) Drawings	500
		(g) Purchases	1,200
		(h) Telephone	600
		(j) Stationery	157

PRACTICE ANSWERS: SECTION 2

25 WIGGLE POGGLE LTD

Discount Allowed

Date 20XX	Details	Amount £	Date 20XX	Details	Amount £
01 July	Balance b/d	1,560			
14 July	SLCA	480			
16 July	SLCA	120	31 July	Balance c/d	2,160
	Total	2,160		Total	2,160
01 Aug	Balance b/d	2,160			

Interest Income

Date 20XX	Details	Amount £	Date 20XX	Details	Amount £
			01 July	Balance b/d	320
31 July	Balance c/d	400	28 July	Bank	80
	Total	400		Total	400
			01 Aug	Balance b/d	400

26 INTREPID INTERIORS

Account name	Amount £	Debit ✔	Credit ✔
Cash at bank	7,250	✔	
Bank Loan	5,000		✔
Capital	10,625		✔
Motor Vehicles	4,750	✔	
Insurances	575	✔	
Stationery	300	✔	
Sundry expenses	225	✔	
Motor expenses	135	✔	
Advertising	990	✔	
Rent and rates	1,400	✔	

27 MONSTER MUNCHIES

(a)

Details	Amount £	Debit ✓	Credit ✓
Balance of debtors at 1 June	48,000	✓	
Goods sold on credit	12,415	✓	
Receipts from credit customers	22,513		✓
Discounts allowed	465		✓
Sales returns from credit customers	320		✓

(b) Dr £37,117 ✓

(c)

	£
Sales ledger control account balance as at 30 June	37,117
Total of sales ledger accounts as at 30 June	36,797
Difference	320

(d) Sales returns may have been entered in the subsidiary ledger x 2 ✓

28 CILLA'S SINKS

(a)

Details	Amount £	Debit ✓	Credit ✓
Balance of creditors at 1 June	52,150		✓
Goods bought on credit	19,215		✓
Payments made to credit suppliers	19,073	✓	
Discounts received	284	✓	
Goods returned to credit suppliers	1,023	✓	

(b) Cr £50,985 ✓

(c)

	£
Purchase ledger control account balance as at 30 June	50,985
Total of purchase ledger accounts as at 30 June	52,008
Difference	1,023

(d) Goods returned may have been omitted from the subsidiary ledger ✓

29 BANK LEDGER

(a)

Bank

	£		£
Capital	10,000	Computer	1,000
Sales	2,000	Telephone	567
Sales	3,000	Rent	1,500
Sales	2,000	Rates	125
		Stationery	247
		Petrol	49
		Purchases	2,500
		Drawings	500
		Petrol	42
		Balance c/d	10,470
	17,000		17,000
Balance b/d	10,470		

(b) A balance b/d on the debit side indicates an asset, i.e. a **positive** bank balance.

30 SALES DAY BOOK

Main ledger accounts

Sales ledger control account

	£		£
26 April SDB	657.60		

Sales account

	£		£
		26 April SDB	548.01

VAT account

	£		£
		26 April SDB	109.59

Subsidiary ledger accounts

J T Howard — SL15

	£		£
22 April SDB 4671	141.89		

F Parker — SL07

	£		£
22 April SDB 4672	101.18		

Harlow Ltd — SL02

	£		£
23 April SDB 4673	127.76		

Edmunds & Co — SL13

	£		£
24 April SDB 4674	171.32		

Peters & Co — SL09

	£		£
26 April SDB 4675	115.45		

31 SALES DAY BOOK (2)

Main ledger accounts

Sales ledger control account

	£		£
		30/4 SRDB	143.19

Sales returns

	£		£
30/4 SRDB	119.32		

VAT account

	£		£
30/4 SRDB	23.87		

Subsidiary ledger accounts

Gerard & Co — G01

	£			£
		7/4	SRDB 2114	35.10

Filmer Ltd — F02

	£			£
		15/4	SRDB 2115	45.88

T Harrison — H04

	£			£
		20/4	SRDB 2116	24.96

Rolls Ltd — R01

	£			£
		28/4	SRDB 2117	37.25

32 PURCHASES RETURNS DAY BOOK

Main ledger

Purchases ledger control account

		£			£
19/4	PRDB	250.32	12/4	Balance b/d	12,678.57

VAT account

	£			£
		12/4	Balance b/d	1,023.90
		19/4	PRDB	41.72

Purchases returns

	£			£
		12/4	Balance b/d	1,818.43
		19/4	PRDB	208.60

Subsidiary ledger

F Williams   PL06

		£			£
18/4	PRDB C4772	168.00	12/4	Balance b/d	673.47

K Bartlett   PL13

		£			£
19/4	PRDB 06638	54.24	12/4	Balance b/d	421.36

J D Withers   PL16

		£			£
15/4	PRDB C0179	28.08	12/4	Balance b/d	446.37

33 COMBINED PURCHASES AND PURCHASE RETURNS DAY BOOK

JOURNAL ENTRY		No: 0254	
Prepared by: A N OTHER			
Authorised by:			
Date: 12/3/X1			
Narrative: To post the purchases day book to the main ledger			
Account		Debit	Credit
Purchases		1,117.26	
VAT		211.2	
Purchase ledger control			1,267.14
Purchase returns			61.32
TOTALS		1,328.46	1,328.46

PRACTICE ANSWERS: SECTION 2

Subsidiary ledger

ABG Ltd   **PL02**

		£			£
12/3	PDB CN477	49.34	5/3	Balance b/d	486.90
			10/3	PDB 016127	298.81

Forker & Co   **PL07**

		£			£
10/3	PDB C4366	24.24	5/3	Balance b/d	503.78
			8/3	PDB 11675	211.66

Print Co   **PL08**

	£			£
		5/3	Balance b/d	229.56
		9/3	PDB 46251	234.94

Homer Ltd   **PL12**

	£			£
		5/3	Balance b/d	734.90
		8/3	PDB 06121	228.64
		11/3	PDB 06132	193.37

G Greg   **PL19**

	£			£
		5/3	Balance b/d	67.89
		11/3	PDB 77918	173.30

MAKING AND RECEIVING PAYMENTS

34 CREDIT SIDE OF THE CASH BOOK

(a) **General ledger**

Account name	Amount £	Debit ✓	Credit ✓
Stationery expense	80	✓	
Repairs	200	✓	
VAT	56	✓	
Cash/bank	336		✓

(b) **Sales ledger**

Account name	Amount £	Debit ✓	Credit ✓
BBG Ltd	7,200		✓
BBG Ltd	180		✓
EFG Ltd	5,000		✓

(c) **General ledger**

Account name	Amount £	Debit ✓	Credit ✓
Cash	12,200	✓	
Discounts allowed	180	✓	
Sales ledger control	12,380		✓

35 ABC LTD

(a) **Cash-book – credit side**

Details	Discount	Cash	Bank	VAT	Payables	Cash purchases	Repairs and Renewals
Balance b/f							
S. Lampard		216		36		180	
S. Bobbins		264		44		220	
Penny Rhodes		530				530	
Henley's Ltd	125		4,925		4,925		
Epic Equipment Maintenance			480	80			400
Total	125	1,010	5,405	160	4,925	930	400

(b) **Cash book – debit side**

Details	Discount	Cash	Bank	Receivables
Balance b/f		1,550	7,425	
D. Davies			851	851
E. Denholm	25		450	450
Total	25	1,550	8,726	1,301

(c) £540

(d) £3,321

(e) Debit

36 CHEQUES FROM DEBTORS

(a) **Cash receipts book**

Date	Narrative	SL Code	Total	VAT	SLCA	Cash sales	Discount
			£	£	£	£	£
20X1							
28/4	G Heilbron	SL04	108.45		108.45		
	L Tessa	SL15	110.57		110.57		3.31
	J Dent	SL17	210.98		210.98		6.32
	F Trainer	SL21	97.60		97.60		
	A Winter	SL09	105.60		105.60		3.16
	Cash sales		265.08	44.18		220.90	
			898.28	44.18	633.20	220.90	12.79

(b) **Main ledger**

VAT account

	£			£
		28/4	CRB	44.18

Sales ledger control account

	£			£
		28/4	CRB	633.20
			CRB – discount	12.79

Sales account

	£			£
		28/4	CRB	220.90

Discount allowed account

		£		£
28/4	CRB	12.79		

(c) **Subsidiary ledger**

G Heilbron   SL04

	£			£
		28/4	CRB	108.45

L Tessa   SL15

	£			£
		28/4	CRB	110.57
			CRB – discount	3.31

J Dent   SL17

	£			£
		28/4	CRB	210.98
			CRB – discount	6.32

F Trainer   SL21

	£			£
		28/4	CRB	97.60

A Winter   SL09

	£			£
		28/4	CRB	105.60
			CRB – discount	3.16

37 CHEQUE LISTING FOR YOUR ORGANISATION

(a) **Cash receipts book**

Date	Narrative	SL Code	Total	VAT	SLCA	Cash sales	Discount
20X1			£	£	£	£	£
15/5	McCaul & Partners	M04	147.56		147.56		2.95
	Dunn Assocs	D02	264.08		264.08		
	P Martin	M02	167.45		167.45		
	F Little	L03	265.89		265.89		7.97
	D Raine	R01	158.02		158.02		3.95
	Cash sales		446.50	74.42		372.08	
			1,449.50	74.42	1,003.00	372.08	14.87

(Note that the total of the 'Discount' column is not included in the cross-cast total of £1,449.50. The discounts allowed are entered into the cash receipts book on a memorandum basis; the total at the end of each period is posted to the sales ledger control account and to an expense account.)

(b) **Main ledger**

VAT account

	£				£
		15/5	CRB		74.42

Sales ledger control account

	£				£
		15/5	CRB		1,003.00
		15/5	CRB – discount		14.87

Sales account

	£				£
		15/5	CRB		372.08

Discount allowed

		£		£
15/5	CRB	14.87		

(c) **Subsidiary ledger**

McCaul & Partners

	£			£
		15/5	CRB	147.56
		15/5	CRB – discount	2.95

Dunn Associates

	£			£
		15/5	CRB	264.08

P Martin

	£			£
		15/5	CRB	167.45

F Little

	£			£
		15/5	CRB	265.89
		15/5	CRB – discount	7.97

D Raine

	£			£
		15/5	CRB	158.02
		15/5	CRB – discount	3.95

38 CHEQUE LISTING FOR A BUSINESS

Cash payments book

Date	Details	Code	Total	VAT	PLCA	Cash purchases	Discounts
			£	£	£	£	£
12/3/X1	Homer Ltd	PL12	168.70		168.70		5.06
	Forker & Co	PL07	179.45		179.45		5.38
	Purchases		334.87	55.81		279.06	
	Print Ass.	PL08	190.45		190.45		
	ABG Ltd	PL02	220.67		220.67		6.62
	Purchases		193.87	32.31		161.56	
	G Greg	PL19	67.89		67.89		
			1,355.90	88.12	827.16	440.62	17.06

Main ledger

Purchases ledger control account

		£			£
12/3	CPB	827.16	5/3	Balance b/d	4,136.24
12/3	CPB – discount	17.06			

VAT account

		£			£
12/3	CPB	88.12	5/3	Balance b/d	1,372.56

Purchases account

		£			£
5/3	Balance b/d	20,465.88			
12/3	CPB	440.62			

Discounts received account

		£			£
			5/3	Balance b/d	784.56
			12/3	CPB	17.06

Subsidiary ledger

ABG Ltd — PL02

		£			£
12/3	CPB 03652	220.67	5/3	Balance b/d	486.90
12/3	CPB – discount	6.62			

Forker & Co — PL07

		£			£
12/3	CPB 03649	179.45	5/3	Balance b/d	503.78
12/3	CPB – discount	5.38			

Print Associates — PL08

		£			£
12/3	CPB 03651	190.45	5/3	Balance b/d	229.56

Homer Ltd — PL12

		£			£
12/3	CPB 03648	168.70	5/3	Balance b/d	734.90
12/3	CPB – discount	5.06			

G Greg — PL19

		£			£
12/3	CPB 03654	67.89	5/3	Balance b/d	67.89

39 CHEQUE PAYMENT

Cash payments book

Date	Details	PL Code	Total £	VAT £	Creditors £	Cash purchases £	Discounts £
8 May	G Rails	PL04	177.56		177.56		4.43
	L Jameson	PL03	257.68		257.68		7.73
	Purchases		216.43	36.07		180.36	
	K Davison	PL07	167.89		167.89		
	T Ives	PL01	289.06		289.06		5.79
	Purchases		263.78	43.96		219.82	
	H Samuels	PL02	124.36		124.36		
			1,496.76	80.03	1,016.55	400.18	17.95

JOURNAL ENTRY		No: 1468	
Prepared by:	A N OTHER		
Authorised by:			
Date:	8 May 20X1		
Narrative:			
To post the cash payments book for the week ending 8 May 20X1			
Account		Debit	Credit
Purchases ledger control		1,016.55	
VAT		80.03	
Purchases		400.18	
Bank			1,496.76
Purchases ledger control		17.95	
Discount received			17.95
TOTALS		1,514.71	1,514.71

Subsidiary ledger

		T Ives			PL01
		£			£
8 May	CPB 001225	289.06	1 May	Balance b/d	332.56
8 May	CPB – discount	5.79			

		H Samuels			PL02
		£			£
8 May	CPB 001227	124.36	1 May	Balance b/d	286.90

		L Jameson			PL03
		£			£
8 May	CPB 001222	257.68	1 May	Balance b/d	623.89
8 May	CPB – discount	7.73			

		G Rails			PL04
		£			£
8 May	CPB 001221	177.56	1 May	Balance b/d	181.99
8 May	CPB – discount	4.43			

		K Davison			PL07
		£			£
8 May	CPB 001224	167.89	1 May	Balance b/d	167.89

LEVEL 1: CERTIFICATE IN BASIC BOOKKEEPING

40 PAPERBOX LTD

Task 1

For the credit of	Paperbox Ltd		To be retained by receiving bank		
Cheques etc for collection to be included in total credit of £ 2,489.87 paid in 19/2/20X0.					
	£	brought forward	£1,099.70	brought forward	£1,876.81
N J Peal	291.60	Pearce & Fellows	659.18	R F Wholesalers Ltd	539.50
Stationery Supplies	245.30	Abraham Matthews Ltd	117.93		
Candle Company Ltd	562.80			Credit Card Voucher	73.56
Carried forward	£1,099.70	carried forward	£1,876.81	Total cheques etc	£2,489.87

Date 19/02/X0
Cashier's stamp and initials

56 – 28 – 48

FINANCIAL BANK PLC
GREENOCK

£50 Notes		
£20 Notes		
£10 Notes		
£5 Notes		
£2 Coins		
£1 Coins		
50p		
20p		
Silver		
Bronze		
Total Cash	–	
Cheques, POs etc	2,489	87
TOTAL £	2,489	87

Fee

No Chqs 6

Paid in by _____

Address/Ref No. _____

Please do not pin or staple this voucher as this will affect the machine processing.

All sales vouchers must be deposited within three banking days of the dates shown on them.

If you are submitting more than 26 vouchers please enclose a separate listing.

If a voucher contravenes the terms of the retailer agreement then the amount shown on the voucher may be charged back to your bank account, either direct or via your paying in branch.

Similarly, if the total amount shown on the Retail Voucher Summary does not balance with our total of vouchers, the difference will be credited (or debited) to your bank account.

SALES VOUCHERS   TOTAL

	£	p
1	22	60
2	5	83
3	26	18
4	18	95
5		
6		
7		
8		
9		
10		
11		
12		
13		
14		
15		
16		
17		
18		
19		
20		
21		
TOTAL	73	56

PRACTICE ANSWERS: SECTION 2

Task 2

Cash Book Receipts

Date	Narrative	Total	SLCA	Mail Order Sales	Other	VAT	Discount allowed
19/2/X0	N J Peal	291.60	291.60				
	Stationery Supplies	245.30	245.30				5.01
	Candle Company Ltd	562.80	562.80				4.95
	Pearce & Fellows	659.18	659.18				13.45
	Abraham Matthews Ltd	117.93	117.93				
	K B Smith	22.60		18.83		3.77	
	R Jones	5.83		4.86		0.97	
	C Bastok	26.18		21.82		4.36	
	J Rirolli	18.95		15.79		3.16	
	R F Wholesalers Ltd (Rent)	539.50			539.50		
	Totals	2,489.87	1,876.81	61.30	539.50	12.26	23.41

Task 3

Journal no: 106
Date: 19/2/X0
Prepared by: A N Other

Code	Account	Debit		Credit	
601	Cash at bank (deposit)	2,489	87		
102	Sales mail order			61	30
202	Bank interest				
504	Sales ledger control account			1,876	81
605	VAT control account			12	26
203	Rent			539	50
409	Discounts allowed	23	41		
504	Sales ledger control account			23	41
Total		2,513	28	2,513	28

THE TRIAL BALANCE

41 SMITH & SON

Account name	Amount £	Debit £	Credit £
Fixtures and Fittings	8,250	8,250	
Capital	18,400		18,400
Bank overdraft	4,870		4,870
Petty cash control	350	350	
Sales ledger control	42,870	42,870	
Purchases ledger control	23,865		23,865
VAT owed to tax authorities	10,245		10,245
Stock	9,870	9,870	
Loan from bank	22,484		22,484
Sales	180,264		180,264
Sales returns	5,420	5,420	
Purchases	129,030	129,030	
Purchases returns	2,678		2,678
Discount allowed	2,222	2,222	
Discount received	3,432		3,432
Heat and Light	1,490	1,490	
Motor expenses	2,354	2,354	
Wages	42,709	42,709	
Rent and rates	10,600	10,600	
Repairs	3,020	3,020	
Hotel expenses	1,890	1,890	
Telephone	2,220	2,220	
Delivery costs	1,276	1,276	
Miscellaneous expenses	2,667	2,667	
Totals	**532,476**	**266,238**	**266,238**

42 EXPIALIDOCIOUS LTD

Account name	Amount £	Debit £	Credit £
Capital	25,360		25,360
Petty cash control	250	250	
Loan from bank	11,600		11,600
Sales ledger control	159,242	159,242	
Purchases ledger control	83,682		83,682
Motor vehicles	35,900	35,900	
Stock	28,460	28,460	
Bank overdraft	10,063		10,063
VAT owing from tax authorities	15,980	15,980	
Purchases	343,014	343,014	
Purchases returns	1,515		1,515
Wages	56,150	56,150	
Motor expenses	2,950	2,950	
Interest income	400		400
Sales	532,900		532,900
Sales returns	5,760	5,760	
Stationery	1,900	1,900	
Light & heat	6,500	6,500	
Discount received	200		200
Discount allowed	2,160	2,160	
Interest paid on overdraft	550	550	
Travel	1,800	1,800	
Marketing	650	650	
Telephone	1,510	1,510	
Miscellaneous expenses	2,944	2,944	
Totals		**665,720**	**665,720**

LEVEL I: CERTIFICATE IN BASIC BOOKKEEPING

43 RICK'S RACERS

	Balances at 1 July	
	Debit £	Credit £
Motor vehicles	24,200	
Plant and Equipment	22,350	
Stock	9,000	
Cash at Bank	11,217	
Cash	150	
Sales ledger control	131,275	
Purchases ledger control		75,336
VAT owing to tax authorities		15,127
Capital		26,247
Bank Loan		12,500
Sales		276,132
Purchases	152,476	
Wages	35,465	
Motor expenses	3,617	
Repairs and Renewals	2,103	
Rent and rates	3,283	
Light and Heat	4,012	
Insurance	4,874	
Sundry Expenses	1,320	
Suspense account (credit balance)		
Total	405,342	405,342

44 CB INTERIOR'S

(a) **Suspense account**

Account name	Amount £	Debit ✓	Credit ✓
Purchase Ledger Control	8,640		✓
Suspense	8,640	✓	

(b) **Removal of incorrect entry**

Account name	Amount £	Debit ✓	Credit ✓
Repairs	750	✓	
Bank	750		✓

Recording of correct entry

Account name	Amount £	Debit ✓	Credit ✓
Repairs	750	✓	
Bank	750		✓

45 JUNIPER JUNGLE'S

(a)

Account name	Amount £	Debit ✓	Credit ✓
Suspense	14,363		✓

(b)

Error in the general ledger	Error disclosed by the trial balance	Error NOT disclosed by the trial balance
Incorrectly calculating the balance on the Motor Vehicles account	✓	
Recording a receipt for commission received in the bank interest received account		✓
Recording a bank receipt for bank interest received on the debit side of both the bank account and the bank interest received account	✓	
Recording supplier invoices on the debit side of the purchase ledger control account and the credit side of the purchases account		✓
Recording a payment by cheque to a payable in the purchase ledger control account only	✓	
Recording a bank payment of £124 for insurance as £142 in the insurance account and £124 in the bank account	✓	

46 TRIAL BALANCE

Trial balance at 31 May 20X1

	£	£
Purchases	385,800	
Creditors		32,000
Computer	8,000	
Motor car	19,200	
Discount received		3,850
Telephone	4,320	
Sales returns	6,720	
Wages	141,440	
VAT		7,200
Drawings	60,000	
Discount allowed	6,400	
Rent and rates	26,200	
Debtors	53,500	
Motor expenses	7,700	
Sales		642,080
Stock	38,880	
Inland Revenue		3,800
Purchases returns		2,560
Electricity	6,080	
Bank	1,920	
Capital		74,670
	766,160	766,160

47 LEDGER ACCOUNTS

Capital account

		£				£
			1 Mar	Bank		12,000

Bank account

		£			£
1 Mar	Capital	12,000	2 Mar	Motor car	4,500
7 Mar	Sales	3,000	2 Mar	Purchases	2,400
20 Mar	Sales	2,100	14 Mar	Rent	600
26 Mar	Debtors	3,800	18 Mar	Stationery	200
			25 Mar	Creditors	3,100
			28 Mar	Drawings	1,600
			31 Mar	Balance c/d	8,500
		20,900			20,900
1 Apr	Balance b/d	8,500			

PRACTICE ANSWERS: SECTION 2

Motor car account

		£			£
2 Mar	Bank	4,500			

Purchases account

		£			£
2 Mar	Bank	2,400			
4 Mar	Creditors	2,500			
12 Mar	Creditors	4,100	31 Mar	Balance c/d	9,000
		9,000			9,000
1 Apr	Balance b/d	9,000			

Purchase ledger control account

		£			£
25 Mar	Bank	3,100	4 Mar	Purchases	2,500
31 Mar	Balance c/d	3,500	12 Mar	Purchases	4,100
		6,600			6,600
			1 Apr	Balance b/d	3,500

Sales account

		£			£
			7 Mar	Bank	3,000
			10 Mar	Debtors	4,600
			15 Mar	Debtors	3,500
31 Mar	Balance c/d	13,200	20 Mar	Bank	2,100
		13,200			13,200
			1 Apr	Balance b/d	13,200

Sales ledger control account

		£			£
10 Mar	Sales	4,600	26 Mar	Bank	3,800
15 Mar	Sales	3,500	31 Mar	Balance c/d	4,300
		8,100			8,100
1 Apr	Balance b/d	4,300			

Rent account

		£		£
14 Mar	Bank	600		

Stationery account

		£		£
18 Mar	Bank	200		

Drawings account

		£		£
28 Mar	Bank	1,600		

Trial balance at 31 March

	£	£
Capital		12,000
Bank	8,500	
Motor car	4,500	
Purchases	9,000	
Purchase ledger control		3,500
Sales		13,200
Sales ledger control	4,300	
Rent	600	
Stationery	200	
Drawings	1,600	
	28,700	28,700

PRACTICE ANSWERS: SECTION 2

UNDERPINNING KNOWLEDGE

48 PURCHASES

(a) No.

(b) Although, by definition, since the stapler will last a few years, it might seem to be a fixed asset, its treatment would come within the remit of the concept of materiality and would probably be treated as office expenses.

49 ENGINE REPAIR

Revenue expenditure.

This is a repair rather than an improvement to an asset. It maintains the level of operation, rather than increasing it so all it does is restore the asset to its ordinary working condition (which therefore supports its current valuation).

50 ACCOUNTING EQUATION

(a)
Assets less capital are equal to liabilities	**True**
Assets plus liabilities are equal to capital	**False**
Capital plus liabilities are equal to assets	**True**

(b) **Classification**

Item	Asset	Liability
	✔	✔
Stock	✔	
Machinery	✔	
5 year loan		✔
Vehicle used by a business	✔	
VAT owed to the tax authorities		✔
Debtors	✔	
Creditors		✔

51 CAPITAL VS. REVENUE

Item	Capital income	Revenue income	Capital expenditure	Revenue expenditure
Receipt from sale of motor vehicle	✓			
Purchase of machinery			✓	
Payment of electricity bill				✓
Purchase of goods for resale				✓
Receipts from cash sales		✓		
Receipts from debtors		✓		
Payments of salaries to staff				✓

52 BLOSSOM BLOOMS

(a) **Payment checks**

Checks to be made	Cheque	Telephone credit card payment
Check expiry date		✓
Check issue number	✓	✓
Check not post-dated		✓
Check security number	✓	
Check words and figures match		✓
Check card has not been tampered with	✓	✓

(b) **True or false**

When Blossom Blooms makes payments to suppliers by debit card, the amount paid affects the bank current account

True

When Blossom Blooms makes payments to suppliers by credit card, the amount paid affects the bank current account

False

53 B

As the manufacturer provides rather than asks for information.

PRACTICE ANSWERS: SECTION 2

54 A

The delivery note lists the goods supplied. It does not include any costs.

55 B

Follows the order of a purchase from a supplier.

56 B

The supplier will issue a credit note to their customer.

57 D

This omission would require an adjustment, say by debit note, to increase the amount to be paid.

58 B

59 C

60 When a company holds personal data about an individual, the company has to comply with the data protection principles. These include not disclosing personal data to others. Therefore, you cannot tell the bank manager any details. If you did, Donald Snow has the right to legal action against you.

61 B

This facilitates the payments and receipts between customers and suppliers between their different banks.

62 A

Every bank customer has his or her own bank account number.

63 D

John is making the payment direct from his bank account to his daughter's and has control over it. If his daughter was claiming the amount it would be a direct debit. BACS is used by companies rather than individuals.

64 B

The partnership has, in effect, not paid the amount due and is still liable to pay it. No one else takes over liability without a separate agreement.

LEVEL I: CERTIFICATE IN BASIC BOOKKEEPING

65 **C**

Consistency causes potential difficulty. For example, if criminals become aware that the same person deals with the banking all the time they could apply pressure on him or her in some way.

66

	Cheque no.	Amount £	Signed by:
(a)	11723	5,379.20	any two of the three directors
(b)	11724	1,406.29	T Tims and S Simon, the managers
(c)	11725	293.50	either T Tims or S Simon
(d)	11726	20,501.80	F Freud, the managing director and G Gammage, the finance director

67 **A**

Provides instances when a bank is entitled to return the cheque. If it is six months out of date it may be that the underlying contract has been resolved in another way and the cheque has been forgotten about. An unsigned cheque may indicate carelessness or a decision not to make payment. Banks agree to pay cheques up to the balance of the customer's account or an agreed credit facility but not beyond so if there are insufficient funds on the account it is entitled to return the cheque. A payee who pays in an 'account payee' cheque is following the instructions written on the cheque.

68 Consideration is defined as:

'an act or forbearance (or the promise of it) on the part of one party to a contract as the price made to him by the other party to the contract'.

An alternative and shorter definition of consideration is that it is 'some benefit to the promisor or detriment to the promisee'. It is important to note, however, that both elements stated in that definition are not required to be present to support a legally enforceable agreement.

The requirement is that for a simple promise to be enforced in the courts as a binding contract, it is necessary that the person to whom the promise was made, i.e. the promisee, should have done something in return for the promise. That something done, or to be done, constitutes consideration.

Consideration can be understood, therefore, as the price paid for a promise.

PRACTICE ANSWERS: SECTION 2

69 (a) **Offer**

An offer sets out the terms upon which an individual is willing to enter into a binding contractual relationship with another person. It is a promise to be bound on particular terms, which is capable of acceptance.

The essential factor to emphasise about an offer is that it may, through acceptance by the offeree, result in a legally enforceable contract. The person who makes the offer is the offeror; the person who receives the offer is the offeree.

Offers, once accepted, may be legally enforced. They must be capable of acceptance and it should be distinguished from mere statements of intention and the supply of information.

(b) **Invitation to treat**

Invitations to treat are distinct from offers in that rather than being offers to others, they are in fact invitations to others to make offers. The person to whom the invitation to treat is made becomes the actual offeror, and the maker of the invitation becomes the offeree. An essential element of this relationship is that the offeree is not bound to accept any offers subsequently made to them.

70 C

Generally advertisements are invitations to treat and not offers. It is the party who responds to the advert who can provide the offer which is then accepted or rejected.

71 C

When an acceptance is communicated by fax machine it is effective on receipt. It is then that a legally binding contract will be recognised. This differs from the postal rule where an acceptance is complete upon posting the acceptance.

72 B

Where a contract is of a social or domestic nature then the courts will assume no intention to be legally bound exists.

73 A

A contract is created immediately upon acceptance of an offer. The contract need not be in written form, and therefore equally no signature need be provided. On payment of the price the contract obligation is completed rather than established at law.

74 C

The innocent party does not solely have the remedy of rescission available to them. They can seek this equitable remedy or seek damages, but not both.

KAPLAN PUBLISHING

75 C

Frustration occurs when performance of a contractual obligation becomes impossible to perform or becomes radically different from that originally anticipated. The fact that performance will take longer and/or will become more expensive does not amount to performance being deemed radically different.

76 C

The response to the offer introduces to the contract something new. It is not a blanket acceptance of that offered. It is a counter-offer and discharges the original offer.

77 C

Consideration need not be adequate. 'Adequacy' relates to monetary value and the courts will not consider this issue, but merely look to enforcing the agreement between the two parties. Both parties must provide consideration which must be sufficient in that it is something the courts recognise irrespective of its value.